20p

ESCAPE FROM
S

ESCAPE FROM THE MOONIES

Susan and Anne Swatland

NEW ENGLISH LIBRARY

A New English Library Original Publication, 1982

First NEL Paperback Edition March 1982

NEL Books are published by
New English Library,
Barnard's Inn, Holborn,
London EC1N 2JR, a division of Hodder and Stoughton Ltd.

Made and printed in Great Britain by Collins, Glasgow

Swatland, Susan

Escape from the Moonies.
1. Unification Church
I. Title
289.9 BX9750.S4

ISBN 0-450-05403-9

This book is dedicated to Joe Alexander, Chris, Dennis, Mark, Matthew, Michael and Virginia, a band described in different ways by different people.

The Moonies called them Agents of Satan.

The police called them Kidnappers.

We prefer to call them Rescuers, modern Knights on White Horses.

Without their courage, without their compassion, there could have been no happy ending.

OUR GRATEFUL THANKS TO:

In England
BERNARD AND LEA, who really understood.
DAPHNE VANE, good counsellor, good friend and a comfort on the dark days.
OUR FAMILY AND FRIENDS, who stood so firm.

In America
DANNY, for his help and loyalty.
HARRY, who gave us the first real hope, a marvellous link.
NEIL MAXWELL, a strong shoulder to lean on when far from home. And all the many people we met at the **REHAB**, for their care and help.

CONTENTS

FOREWORD

by Joe Alexander

ON 17 MARCH, 1981, Moonie convert Susan Swatland was rescued from the streets of San Francisco by a group of men hired by her mother Anne. The story made headlines around the globe. And as a man who has dedicated his days to the rescue of young people from pseudo religious movements, I welcomed those stories. The world is awakening all too slowly to the menace that these cults pose to our children. Many of their leaders are sinister in the extreme and the Rev Sun Myung Moon, founder of the Unification Church, is the daddy of them all.

I would do nothing at all to prevent a son of mine following the messiah of his choosing provided he was allowed to do so of his own free-will. But the Unification Church doesn't work that way.

Young men and women, many of them on holiday and far from home, are lured into the Moonies by deceit and downright fraud. No one tells them that their new-found friends belong to a cult. No one tells them that the farm they're invited to for the weekend is an indoctrination centre. No one tells them that they will be taught to regard their parents as Satanic. And you can be sure that no one ever tells them they will eventually be working up to twenty hours a day to enable Moon and his fellow leaders to continue living in the style to which they have become accustomed . . . in millionaire mansions surrounded by servants, bodyguards and just about everything that big money can buy.

The cult robs its followers of their possessions, their identities and their minds. They become robots programmed to follow the commands of their self-styled Messiah.

The brainwashing technique is basically the same as that practised on American prisoners of war in Korea.

It is terrifyingly effective. And so at the end of the day anguished parents face the stark choice that eventually came to Anne and Michael Swatland. Should they accept their loss, sit back, do nothing and allow their daughter to be enslaved by the cult? Or should they rescue her to freedom? As loving, caring parents, there could only be one answer. They would be less than parents should they fail to do so.

Over the years I have been threatened many times by members of the Unification Church. I have been warned to choose my words carefully. So being an open-minded man I will do just that. I will state my views with considerable care. I consider the cult to be a threat to all the freedoms we hold most dear. I consider Sun Myung Moon to be a charlatan who waxes rich on the goodness and the ideals of the young. I consider his followers to be the innocent victims of their own dreams for a better world. And above all else I consider them victims of the Millionaire Messiah.

In this mother-and-daughter book, both Anne and Susan give their separate versions of the eight traumatic months which threatened to tear the family apart. But to avoid any confusion, the words belong to Susan unless stated otherwise.

PREFACE

IT ALL happened so fast. A car stopped just behind me. There were the sounds of doors opening and of running feet followed by Suzanne's piercing scream. Before I could move, two big men had seized me. One wrapped his arms around my chest, the other grabbed my legs; and suddenly I was being carried, struggling, screaming across the pavement and into the back of the car.

I cried out, 'Someone help me, someone help me. Get the police. I'm being kidnapped.' But it was like a tableau. The passers-by on that street in San Francisco just stood there, frozen by the speed of the attack. I was still fighting even though they had me stretched out across the back seat. A huge long-haired, bearded man was pinning down my shoulders; while the other, handsome as any film star, had a tight hold on my legs, but I'd locked those legs against the door so that it couldn't be closed.

The car began to move with Suzanne running alongside, holding on to the door, still screaming. 'Let go, honey,' said the bruiser with the film star looks, 'or you'll hurt yourself.' And if I hadn't known better I might have imagined that there was a touch of concern in his voice. Then they were accelerating away, leaving Suzanne behind; and soon her distant wail faded into the morning air.

This was the spectre that had haunted so many of my dreams. Over and over again the Moonies had warned us about these agents of Satan. So I had no illusions about the kind of fate that awaited me. Most of the other kidnapped sisters had been tied up and tortured. Several had been stripped and raped. I still had my feet wedged against the door and the handsome one was holding on with his free hand to prevent it flying open.

He turned to me and said, 'It's all right, Sue, your mother's here.'

I stopped struggling for the first time and looked towards the front seat. I had been vaguely conscious of the fact that a woman was sitting next to the driver, but hadn't gained any real impression. Even now she didn't look like my mother. This woman was wearing some strange rain hat and my mother had never liked hats. I remembered her walking bareheaded in both the wind and the rain. This woman was wearing dark glasses and this too was something I'd never seen my mother do. But now she took them off and I realised they were part of a disguise. She had lost weight since last we'd met, was pale and looking terribly tired.

'I'm sorry, Sue darling,' she said and at least the voice hadn't changed. 'We didn't want to take you by force, but in the end there was no other choice.'

At that moment I came as close to hatred for my mother as I had ever been in my life before. I found it incredible that she had done this terrible thing to me. Yet it proved that the Moonies had been right all along.

They had always said that parents could never be trusted; that at the very best they were misguided. I had clung to the faith that my parents would be rather more understanding than most. Now they had betrayed that trust by hiring a band of professional kidnappers.

'How could you possibly get involved with such evil men?' I asked her. At this, the thugs smiled their Satanic smiles.

But my mother speaking very quietly said, 'I have been with these men for a week now and believe me they're good men, and kind men.'

For the moment words were beyond me. My mother had lived her life in the country away from the big cities, but she had always been sensible, never naïve like this. How could she possibly describe criminals for hire as 'good men'? . . . people who made a living from brutality and torture as 'kind'?

I made another attempt to make her see the truth. 'How much are you paying them?' I asked.

Normally that kind of question asked in front of strangers would have embarrassed her, but she merely shrugged. 'Not much,' she said matter-of-factly. 'Just enough to cover their expenses. You have to understand, Sue, we all want to help you.'

I didn't know whether she was telling the truth about the money; but even if she was, it did nothing to wash away my fears. We had been told that most of these men were motivated solely by greed and demanded huge sums from parents they'd hoodwinked. However there were even worse bands of men who did the job cheaply so that they could enjoy the sadistic kicks. I expected to be hurt. That was inevitable. But I didn't want to be humiliated.

So I looked into my mother's eyes and asked, 'Will you stay beside me all the time? These people are evil. but they won't harm me while you're around.'

'I'll never leave you,' she promised. 'I'll always be with you.'

Having become passive, I was allowed to sit upright on the back seat between the two men. The initial shock of being kidnapped had gone and I was already beginning to make my plans. My mother's promise to stay by my side had bought me maybe two days; and so I must try to make my escape during those two days. For it could only be a matter of time before these thugs thought up a trick to lure my mother away; and then I would be entirely at their mercy.

I looked at the men from the corner of my eyes and I felt as though I'd seen them all before. They were the spectres who'd haunted my lonely nights. The driver, like the big brute on my left, had long hair; and I'd been told a thousand times that this is the mark of Satan. The handsome one was part of my dreams too. Deprogrammers, the polite name for kidnappers, use sex as a weapon to sweep away spiritual and righteous thoughts. Knowing this, I vowed to hate him even more fiercely than I hated the others, because he posed the greatest threat.

I began to study the landmarks along the way; so that

I would have some idea of where I was about to be kept prisoner. Otherwise escape would be that much more difficult. We went through Chinatown and seemed to be heading towards Los Angeles Airport. I had heard of deprogrammers working at airports, shutting their victims in soundproof chambers for seventy-two hours at a time without either sleep or food, and subjecting them to eardrum bursting noise. It was going to be hell; yet already I was glad that they had taken me and not Suzanne. For I was strong physically and spiritually. I saw it as a chance to test my faith. I knew Heavenly Father would help me so long as I remained firm. But if I began to panic and doubt, then sure enough Satan would get me. So at all costs I must keep my cool, chant, pray and keep out the evil spirits. Satan feeds off doubt and I didn't want him getting fat. I was resentful, but filled with confidence.

I was going to beat these thugs and return to my true family, my brothers and sisters in the Unification Church; and to my true father, the Rev Sun Myung Moon.

Above all else, I wished to defeat the mother who had betrayed me.

Chapter One

THE SPIDER'S WEB

'*It's the saddest thing in the world. People don't trust each other any more.*' Noah Ross, Director of the San Francisco Moonies

I WAS moving towards the close of a perfect day. I had spent most of it with my college friend Diana on the sands of Santa Barbara. We had lazed under the hot Californian sun, swum out into the ocean beyond the surf and shared cokes with students from a dozen different lands. Now with twilight beginning to fall over the city, we were dining in a little Mexican restaurant. The heat of the day still lingered and so everything was very casual. Diana and I, like most of the diners, wore shorts and T-shirts, and there wasn't a jacket or a tie to be seen.

A man in his early twenties was tacking shyly around the floor selling red roses from a basket. He was wearing cotton trousers and a check shirt, but he was the kind who never stands out in the crowd. So I didn't take too much notice of him. Maybe I should have done so; for he was about to change my life, my world.

Eventually he came to our table, smiled and said, 'How about making my day and buying a rose?'

I replied, 'Another time I'd love to; but I've nowhere to pin it and it would look kinda silly on a T-shirt.'

He shrugged and the smile became even warmer as he crouched down beside us, clearly intrigued by my accent.

'What part of England do you come from?' he asked.

We told him we were students from the Chelsea College of Physical Education in Eastbourne; and that we were heading up the west coast of America during our ten weeks' holiday.

'You're a bit like me,' he said. 'I came down here from Canada three years ago and I've enjoyed it so much that I've never gone back. I tour around, but I have a base with some friends in San Francisco.'

Diana who is dark and eye-catching told him we were heading for San Francisco too and he immediately said, 'In that case you must go and see my friends. They'll be really, really happy to meet you.'

He wrote down their address and telephone number and before leaving he said again, 'Now don't forget, please visit my friends. Tell them Eric sent you and you'll be made very welcome.'

He touched our hands gently as though in benediction, sold a couple of roses casually to the people at the next table, waved us goodbye from the doorway and disappeared into the night. I looked at the address. It was 1153 Bush Street which meant nothing at all to me at the time. Very soon it would come to mean a great deal. Eric had neglected to mention that this was the headquarters of the San Francisco Moonies.

Such an offer of hospitality from a complete stranger hadn't surprised us too much. We had been in California for a week and it was as though everyone was determined to make sure we enjoyed our stay. We had spent three days with my American boyfriend Ken and his family at La Jolla just outside San Diego, then moved up the coast to Santa Barbara and all along the way people just couldn't have been more friendly.

We did think about travelling by Greyhound coach to San Francisco; but they move up the big main highways and we decided it would be more fun to hitch a lift up the coastal road. Diana produced a Union Jack handkerchief and in no time at all a truck stopped and two Starsky and Hutch types named Kevin and Rusty were smiling down at us. 'We're heading for Santa Cruz, if that's any help,' they said and gratefully we climbed aboard. We were all in our early twenties and as we went along that roller-coaster road, dipping down into the lush green valleys and climbing to the peaks with their scenic views of the ocean, life seemed very sweet to us. We stopped at cafés along the way and by nightfall we had reached Santa Cruz.

Early the following morning I rang the number Eric had given me in San Francisco. A girl answered and I said, 'We're friends of Eric and he told us we could call round one evening and say "Hello". We were wondering whether it would be okay to crash down on your floor with our sleeping bags.'

There was an awkward silence and I thought maybe I'd said something wrong. But she whispered hesitantly, 'Could you wait a moment,' and went to fetch someone else. Then a man's voice was coming down the line, saying, 'Yes, that will be fine. Eric told us you'd be coming. We're all looking forward to meeting you.'

Three lifts later we were dropped outside 1153 Bush Street, an imposing red-brick Victorian mansion fronted by a wrought-iron gate. I had been expecting something much more humble, more on the lines of the seen-better-days houses where so many English students tend to live in the university towns. We rang the bell and the door was opened by a blonde named Patsy.

'Hi, there,' she said smiling at us with the simple delighted look of a small child, 'what are your names?'

'I'm Sue,' I said, 'and this is Diana.'

'Well come on in,' she said, smiling sweetly. 'Everyone's just dying to meet you.'

We stepped into the carpeted hallway. At least sixty pairs of shoes were lined up neatly, toy soldiers on parade. Before we could ask about this the smiling Patsy was saying, 'Would you mind taking yours off too. We try to save wear on the carpets.'

The Moonies have a favourite phrase called 'Heavenly Deception' which means that it's perfectly all right to lie provided you are doing so for the benefit of the Unification Church (the official title of the Moonies) or more specifically for the benefit of its Messiah, the Rev Sun Myung Moon. This was our first encounter with Heavenly Deception as practised by Patsy. The shoes hadn't been removed for the sake of the carpets. They had been removed to prevent the evil spirits from the streets being brought into a holy house. If we had known that, we would have made hasty excuses and hightailed it out of there. We weren't seeking salvation Korean-style . . . just a holiday in the sun. And I'm sure the same thing applies to the thousands of other innocents who get lured into the spider's web known as Bush Street.

At that first encounter there is no mention of religion, no mention of the Unification Church, and most definitely no mention of the Messianic Moon.

Patsy asked us for a donation and being uncertain what to give we gave a dollar each. From the far end of the hallway we could hear the twanging of a guitar and a deep country voice singing 'The Most Beautiful Girl'. Patsy hummed the tune quietly. 'That's Chris,' she said, 'isn't he super. He's one of the stars of our entertainment. You must meet him later. But come in and listen, you'll enjoy it. I know you will.'

Still with the same sweet smile, she led us to a place in the back row of a large room. As we sat down, people were turning round and smiling at us in the friendliest way. Chris finished with the line, 'If you happen to see her, tell her I'm sorry, tell her I love her,' and there was enthusiastic applause as he stepped down to be replaced by another singing guitar player. This time it was 'High Noon'.

I noticed that as Chris returned to his place, boys and girls alike were reaching out to touch his hand as he walked by. Diana and I were soon joined by an English girl called Carol who had clearly been asked to look after us. During the interval, we were given two omelettes and everyone seemed to be combining to make sure that we had a good time.

At the end of the concert, a burly New Zealander named Doctor John stood up and announced, 'Now we are going to have a talk that explains how we run our community. The speaker is a graduate in philosophy and his name is Noah Ross. During his college days, he was one of the nation's top basketball stars. A hand please for Noah.'

With that a thin, medium-sized man with glasses bounded on to the stage. He was in his early thirties, wearing dark cotton trousers and a white shirt without a jacket. In fact during the eight months I spent with Noah I never once saw him wear a jacket. When it turned cold, he'd slip on a sports V-necked sweater. It was all part of the image he was so anxious to project.

This was why he liked to run up the aisle and leap on to the stage, looking very athletic. It was in keeping with his basketball reputation. Right from the start this puzzled me; for all the top basketball players I'd seen on television had been giants of men; and Noah would have needed bionic heels to even get so much as a touch of the ball. I wondered whether he was maybe yet another Walter Mitty and this his impossible dream. But his manner was so friendly that it didn't seem to matter, indeed it made him appear even more human. Still I might not have felt that way if Doctor John had announced Noah's true title. Noah was Director of the San Francisco Moonies and as such he ranked immediately behind Doctor Mose Durst and his Korean wife Onni in the West Coast hierarchy. On this low-key first evening such information was very definitely taboo.

Noah's style of speaking was smooth, amusing and very professional. He is a natural mimic and his voice can change from that of a small child to full-grown man in the flicker of a second.

He told us the Elephant Story which is one of the Moonie favourites, illustrating the way that humans can study the same object and yet still emerge with different views of the truth.

'There was this huge gentle elephant,' he said, 'surrounded by blind-folded men. The first man grabbed the elephant's tail, gave it a tug and thought he was holding a piece of rope. Another seized the trunk and, as the elephant had just drunk a bucketful of water, he squirted the water all over the man. So this man thought the trunk was a hose. Another man ran into the side of the elephant, spread his hands and thought it was a hairy wall. Another put his arms around the leg and thought it was a tree; and another the tusk and thought it was a horn. So just imagine that this elephant represents the whole of life and you'll understand the parable. All these men were living in their own world believing that their reality was *the* reality. But they had forgotten to take in the entirety of life. Their view was too narrow; and this is why humans are so often blind to the truth.'

He went on to talk about the breakdown in human relationships. 'It's the saddest thing in the world,' he said, 'People don't trust each other any more.' As he was in the process of setting up a band of innocents, that must rank as quite a quote.

He talked about the insensitivity of man. 'If there is a hurricane, a forest fire or storm clouds coming our way, the animals will know about them long before man.'

And as always with Noah there was a story to underline the message. 'A man decided to play a trick on one of his homing pigeons. He put it in the back of a van and drove a hundred miles. He turned the cage around fifty-two times to confuse the bird, changed the magnetic field by putting magnets in the pigeon's wings and then he released it.'

As he was saying this, Noah became the man, peering into the sky, following the pigeon's flight until finally it disappeared from view heading for home. Noah's face reflected the astonishment of the man, then switched to dismay. 'Where am I?' he asked.

After the talk Noah nodded and smiled, pleased by the applause and came bounding down the aisle, once more the keen-eyed star of the basketball arenas.

Doctor John gave us a slide show of Boonville, the Moonies' 650-acre retreat set in the rolling forests of Mendocino County, some hundred and twenty miles to the north of San Francisco. We saw peaceful mountain streams, clean-cut boys walking through the hills, pretty girls at play, a rustic paradise without so much as a car in sight.

He paused seemingly lost in wonder. 'Beautiful, isn't

it,' he said. 'At Boonville, even the cows smile.' He chuckled at his own joke. 'Now we would like to invite you all up to our farm for a two-day seminar so that we can discuss in more detail some of the ideas we've heard tonight. I'm afraid we have to ask for a twenty-dollar donation to cover food and travel. But you're most welcome and I can promise you the most remarkable two days of your life.'

We went into the room next door where tea and coffee were being served and all the time people were coming up to me, smiling, looking deep into my eyes and saying things like, 'Hi. I'm Jake. Lovely to have you with us.'

The fixity of some of those smiles did worry me a little, but they all seemed so sincere that I didn't give it too much thought. I had come from a close-knit, loving family. I'd had plenty of good friends at college. But I had never experienced warmth like this before. It was quite overwhelming. And then Carol was saying, 'Do come to Boonville with us, Sue. It would make me so happy if you would.'

Diana and I had decided a few days earlier that we would like to see an American ranch and this seemed a perfect opportunity. And having been raised on an English farm, I wanted to see how they did it Yankee-style. However just to be safe I said, 'I'll have to check with my friend first.'

At this Carol said quickly, 'Diana has already agreed to come.'

So I shrugged, 'Great, then we'll both come.'

This was another bit of Heavenly Deception. For at that selfsame moment Diana was being told that I was keen to go and was agreeing for the same reason.

An earnest-looking boy with freckles came up to me and said, 'Do you believe in God?' and when I told him 'No', he seemed surprised. 'You seemed such a contented person,' he said sounding disappointed. 'I just assumed you would be religious.'

He made no attempt to pursue the subject, glanced at Carol who had stopped smiling and departed abruptly.

We were asked to sign a form to confirm that we wished to go to Boonville; and if I'd read the small print, I would have seen the words '*Unification Church*'. But you would have needed eagle eyes to spot that at a casual glance.

At nine o'clock everyone who was going to Boonville gathered in a group. Someone twanged a guitar and we all sang 'You Are My Sunshine'.

As soon as the singing stopped, there was another shout, 'How about a choo-choo?' Everyone immediately linked arms and jumped in rhythm to cries of, 'Choo-choo-choo, choo-choo-choo, choo-choo-choo. Yea! Yea! Pow!' Carol had one of my arms and a smiling Adonis had the other. I assumed it was some sort of college chant; and although I considered this rather childish, I wouldn't have said so for the world. They were all so friendly, so well-meaning, that I would have felt like a monster.

We reclaimed our shoes, grabbed our rucksacks and climbed aboard a full-sized ex-public bus. Diana and I sat together and immediately in front sat Carol and her friend Pippa. Carol told us that she had been living in the community for the past three months, and Pippa for the past ten weeks. Both had given up their jobs. I asked them about their parents' reaction to all this; and they shrugged as though it was a matter of no importance. I remember thinking how upset my own parents would have been if I'd decided to give up college; and for the moment that was the very last thought in my mind.

I was feeling very drowsy, so after half-an-hour I went to the back of the bus, stretched out and fell asleep. I woke just after midnight as we began to bump along a rough country road. The headlights of the bus illuminated a sign reading 'BOONVILLE IDEAL CITY RANCH' and close by there was another sign, 'PLEASE DO NOT ENTER WITHOUT PRIOR PERMISSION OF OWNER UNDER PENALTY OF LAW'. An eight-foot high barbed-wire fence surrounded the farm.

We clambered over a rickety suspension bridge. The boys were herded towards a converted hen house called the Chicken Palace and the girls went to a cabin. Strips of foam were spread out on the floor and pausing only to take off our shoes, we slipped fully-dressed into our sleeping bags. I was positioned between Carol and Diana. Someone blew out the storm lantern and then there was only the pale glow of the moon.

I lay awake for a while wondering why a farm would need warning notices and those high barbed-wire fences. I was still wondering when I fell asleep.

Chapter Two

THE LOVE BOMBING

'*We can give you eternal ecstasy . . .*' Bethie, group leader at Boonville

EARLY MORNING sunshine was already coming through the cabin windows as we were woken at seven by the strains of 'The Red, Red, Robin'.

A big girl with a guitar and a good-neighbour smile was standing in the doorway. 'Good morning, everybody,' she shouted. 'How are you?'

'Terrific,' came the thundered reply and the room was filled with smiling faces. Carol was unzipping my sleeping bag, helping me climb out with eager hands.

'Come on, Sue,' she urged, 'this is the best time of the day.'

I stumbled yawning into the sunlight where we all joined hands and sang 'Oh, What a Beautiful Morning'; and indeed it was. There wasn't a cloud in the sky. The rising sun had formed a halo over the trees of the forest. And the hills had been painted gold by the shrubs of summer. We did exercises for half-an-hour, press-ups, stride jumps, jumping Jacks; and although some of the older Moonies lost their smiles, I was enjoying myself in the morning air. We finished with a choo-choo and then Jacob, an amiable Welshman who tipped the scales at just over 200 pounds, stepped out in front of us and said, 'We have a rule at Boonville, no smoking, no drinking and no drugs, because we believe in attaining a natural high. And we would be grateful if you would follow this for the next two days. I can promise you that you'll find it a worthwhile experience.'

We were then divided up into groups of eight, I went into Bethie's group and Diana into Jacob's, supposedly because she was Welsh. But this is standard Moonie policy to separate friends.

They also discourage newcomers from talking to

other newcomers. It encourages negativity, they say.

Bethie was the key figure at Boonville and a remarkable one. She was in her late twenties, fuzzy-haired, thin with rabbit-teeth, Jewish and motherly. She had gained a teacher's degree in anthropology and worked for a while in the psychiatric department of a children's hospital, an experience which had nearly broken her heart. When her boyfriend Matthew wrote to say that he had joined the Moonies, she didn't hesitate. She joined them too. For the past seven years she had been existing on an average of three hours sleep a night, totally dedicated to the task of indoctrinating the constant flow of recruits who passed through her hands, fussing over them like a mother hen. On the occasions when her wiles failed to lure these innocents into the Moonie web, she would stand at the gate as they returned to the outside world, waving them goodbye with tears streaming down her face. And for long afterwards she would mourn for them with a sadness to match that of any mother who has ever lost a child.

It was said that when she first joined the Moonies, she was buxom and bouncy; but the years had taken a terrible toll. The flesh had faded from her bones and now she seemed to be hovering forever on the brink of exhaustion. Bethie probably did more harm to me than anyone else has ever done; for she was the one who cast the spell. But I still look upon her as a misguided and lovely lady, kind and sensitive, and perhaps the greatest victim of them all.

We had breakfast of cereals and fruit under a tree and it gave me my first chance to study these people who had come so suddenly into my life. The boys were clean-cut and wholesome, college-style, with unfashionably short haircuts. The fixity of their smiles and something about their eyes worried me vaguely, but I was becoming accustomed to it. Some of the girls looked very old fashioned in their long dresses, a bit like 'The Little House on The Prairie'; still there wasn't much time for independent thinking at Boonville.

While we were still munching our cornflakes Bethie

was explaining, 'At breakfast we have a custom called Cereal Drama, this means sharing something with each other, some experience that has made us happy or troubled us. This will help us to get to know each other better and so bring us closer together.'

Sharing is another word for confessing and as such an important weapon in the brainwashing armoury of the Moonies. Once a newcomer had divulged some secret sin, this would be later magnified and used to home in on our weak spots, thus creating the much desired feeling of guilt.

'Well, who's going to be the first to share?' asked Bethie brightly and immediately five hands were raised. Mine stayed down. I had been assuming that everyone in Bethie's group had been newcomers, but this wasn't so. There were five old Moonies and only two newcomers, besides myself . . . a Swiss girl called Vrenni and a husky fair-haired boy with mischievous eyes called Barney.

And surprise, surprise, it was the five old Moonies who had their hands raised. That was part of the act. They would confess to the same things over and over again. Each told us a relatively minor thing about his past. Then Bethie turned to me and said, 'Come on, Sue, please tell us something about yourself. We would all love to hear.'

So I told them that I lived on a farm in the south of England, had two younger brothers called Mark and Chris, had spent a term as an exchange student at Brockfort just outside New York and still had a year of my course to complete before I could qualify as a physical education teacher. At this, the Moonies clapped and Bethie gave us her motherly smile.

'I know it isn't easy to share with others just because they want you to; or to sing because it makes others happy. And it's never easy to be a totally unselfish person, to start thinking about the happiness of others before you think of your own.

'But this is what we're doing at Boonville. We are trying to set up a model community where people learn to truly care about one another. Look upon it as a two-day experiment in a different way of living. Some of the things you see here may seem strange to you. But please open your minds and give yourself the chance to understand. You have all known fleeting moments of ecstasy. Well, stay with us for a while. We can give you eternal ecstasy.'

It was heady stuff. We were being shown the gateway to paradise; and if all those smiles truly reflected inner joy, then maybe it wasn't entirely a dream.

Boonville was proving to be a merry-go-round that might slow down from time to time to let people climb on, but never ever stopped. We moved from one activity to the next without pause. There always seemed to be someone holding my hand, talking to me or smiling deep into my eyes. Breakfast was followed by a lecture on evolution which was followed by more sharing; which in its turn was followed by a truck ride out into the fields. Encouraged by Bethie, we sang all the way.

Our task was to weed the Baby's Breath, delicate little white flowers which are used in decorations. The sun was high in the sky; and as I was anxious to build up a tan, I slipped off my T-shirt which left me with shorts and a halter top. Diana stripped down to a bikini which allied with her figure could normally be guaranteed to cause a bit of passing interest. But seemingly not at Boonville. The sight appeared to bring cheer to the heart of Barney; but most of the other boys kept their eyes averted and weeded away more furiously than ever. The older girls looked mildly disapproving and yet no one said a word. Such is the wish to conform that Diana and I, after an uncomfortable hour, decided tacitly that our tans could wait awhile. We put on our T-shirts.

As we weeded, we sang and it reminded me a little of those old-time musicals where the Southern belles are singing in the cotton fields and Paul Robeson is doing the solo bits. Judging by the raucous sounds around me, we were a bit short on Paul Robesons.

Later we went for a swim in the river which had been

dammed up to create a deep pool. To my surprise everyone dived in fully clothed. Even the boys swam in their T-shirts. So anxious not to rock the boat, I kept mine on too. Even while swimming, I was surrounded by smiles; and when I finally returned to the river bank, half a dozen friendly hands reached out to help me.

I had never known so much loving *sans* sex. There always seemed to be somebody holding my hand, hugging me or rubbing the back of my shoulders to keep me awake during lectures. It was what the Moonies call Love Bombing and is a vital part of their Mind Control techniques. So too is the constant singing and chanting which disorientates you from the big, wide, wicked world that lies somewhere out there beyond the barbed-wire of Boonville. Mostly I was enjoying myself. I liked the land and the country air. I was touched by the friendliness of the people. I had enjoyed working in the fields, swimming and the exercises. And as a student I found the lectures intriguing.

But I desperately needed to do a little independent thinking and this was seemingly impossible. That is unless you have the ability to think while you're singing or chanting, doing Jumping Jacks or a choo-choo, looking into an everlasting line of smiling eyes or sharing. You couldn't even cheat during the lectures and let the mind ramble. There was always Bethie, Carol or one of the older girls alongside to make sure my eyes didn't wander even for an instant. At the slightest hint of this there would be a gentle prod and a pleading voice saying, 'Sue, try to listen. This next bit is fascinating. It would be such a shame to miss it.'

The sharing too had become progressively more intimate. One of the boys confessed that in his early teens he had looked at his older sister with lustful eyes. One of the girls had purposely left the bathroom door open so that her stepfather could catch a glimpse of her under the shower; and later in the dark corridor she had allowed him to touch her with careless (or come to think of it, not so careless) hands. The stepfather sounded like a cross between Paul Newman and Dracula.

Another girl had made love to a college professor while his two small children slept in the next room. I had no such steamy stories to tell and Bethie was clearly disappointed.

'But tell us more about your parents, Sue,' she urged. 'Have they always understood you, haven't you ever had any quarrels?'

'Oh sure,' I said, 'we've had the odd falling-out just like any other family.'

'Well, tell us about them,' chorused my new-found friends.

I shrugged. 'They're too petty. I just couldn't remember them.'

And Bethie who had been playing that scene for seven years was wise enough to let it lie. I had no intention of parading family secrets before a band of people who until the dawning of this day had been strangers. Even if I'd wanted to do so, I probably couldn't have remembered anything. I was by then physically and mentally exhausted. The fresh air, the exercise and the legion of new ideas poured into my head had left me numb.

But before I tumbled into my sleeping bag, I was determined to take a shower and at least have a moment to myself. With that thought, I slid away like a thief into the night, stripped and let the warm water cascade over me with a sense of oceanic relief. For the first time that day tranquillity returned. I was lazily soaping my body when I heard a shoe scuff across the floor. I turned to see the smiling face of Carol.

'How have you liked your first day?' she asked. 'Is there anything you don't understand?'

A chilling thought touched me. I had met Carol just thirty hours earlier; and during those thirty hours she had barely left my side for more than a moment at a time. I had gained a shadow. Alarm bells were ringing in the backrooms of my mind; and if I'd listened to them, I could still have left Boonville of my own free-will. But I was too tired for thinking. I just had the strength left to slide into my sleeping bag with Carol, dutiful as ever, zipping me up; and that was the last thing I remembered until the twanging of the guitar and the red, red robin woke me on the dawn of a new day.

It followed the path of the one that had gone before, and out in the fields in the late afternoon, Bethie put her frail arm around me.

'Sue,' she said, 'I feel very close to you. I know you've enjoyed your two days at Boonville. But you've only just begun to learn about our community. So please say you'll come with us to Camp K. It will make me so happy if you do.'

I said, 'I'm travelling with Diana. So it's only fair that I should ask her first. But if she's willing I'd love to come.'

And with the inevitable Heavenly Deception, Bethie replied quickly, 'We've already asked her. She wants to come.'

Just before midnight we boarded a Moonie bus and arrived at Camp K (K for Korea) in the early hours. These late-night journeys are part of a deliberate ploy intended to increase the newcomer's sense of disorientation. I felt as though I was in the middle of nowhere. I presumed we were still in the state of California, but wasn't sure. I didn't even know which was north and which was south.

Where Boonville had been a rustic farm, Camp Korea was virtually an army camp. There were high-wire fences and a guardhouse on the bridge. Life was hard and disciplines fierce. The Moonies reason that by the time you've reached this stage, the battle for your mind has been won. There is less need for discretion or deception. They can pour in the religion with two important reservations. They still don't mention either the name of the Church or the name of the mysterious Messiah.

At one of our first Cereal Dramas in Camp K, Diana confided casually. 'The last thing my mother said to me when I left England was, "Whatever you do, don't get mixed up with the Moonies." ' The silence was deafening.

'Honestly,' said Diana, 'the things mums say.' The echoing laughter of the Moonies had a distinctly hollow ring.

Afterwards, during a rare moment alone with Diana, I asked her who the Moonies were and why her mother was so worried about them.

'I don't really know,' said Diana, 'just a bunch of religious crack-pots I expect.'

Such was the state of our innocence.

Barney was missing from our group and when I questioned Bethie she said, 'He's gone back to the city. He was too negative.'

Her voice was stern, but the eyes gave her away. She had lost another chick from the nest and it hurt.

In the afternoon of the first day at Camp Korea, we were supposed to play a game of dodgeball on the top of the hill. However I'd been wanting to get in touch with my boyfriend Ken; so I told Bethie I wouldn't be playing. I had a letter to write instead.

Instantly her manner changed. 'No,' she said flatly, 'the letter can wait. I think it will be better that you play.'

So I said, 'Please, Bethie, this is a letter to my boyfriend and it's important to me.'

But she was adamant and suddenly I was in tears and Bethie once more the mother hen was wrapping her arms around me and drawing my head to her breast.

'You're just overtired,' she said. 'Forget about the dodgeball, come down to the river for a swim and tell me all about this boyfriend of yours.'

So that's what we did. We went for our swim and I explained how I'd met Ken while we were both students at Brockfort, how I'd stayed with his family and how we were planning to meet up again in New York.

She listened attentively, her head on one side, and then she said, 'Be guided by me, Sue, wait a few more days before you write that letter; and by then you'll have had a chance to sort out your true feelings.'

I agreed meekly enough and I can see now that this

had to be my moment of no return. It was all so out of character.

Firstly I just wasn't the crying kind; and secondly until I'd crossed the threshold of Bush Street, no one in the whole wide world could have dominated me that way.

I never again looked upon my smiling friends as boys and girls. They were brothers and sisters. I accepted the weird, mind-boggling jargon of the cult* as though I'd been taught it from the cradle. And I was accepting the messages from the lectures as pure gospel.

The Moonies look upon letters to boyfriends and parents as a constant source of danger. Jacob gave us a talk on the subject.

'When you write home to your parents,' he counselled, 'don't tell them that you're helping to build the Heavenly Kingdom; because they won't understand and such talk will only alarm them. Just tell them that you are spending a few days with some friends.'

I followed that advice with Bethie guiding my hand. I was equally obedient when I played dodgeball each day, joining in the communal chant, 'Bomb with love . . . Bomb with love . . . Bomb with love.'

Bethie, looking like an animated kewpie doll, would leap up and down driving us into fresh areas of hysteria.

'We're going to beat 'em.' she cried. 'We're going to beat 'em so bad they'll think the sky's fallen down on 'em. And do you know why?'

'Because we love them,' came the thunderous reply.

Considering that dodgeball is a game for mixed teams, it could get surprisingly rough. The idea is to throw the ball as hard as you can at one of your opponents and if you score a hit, they're out of the game. The survivors are the winners. Several of the sisters wound up with bloodied noses; but because of the fervour, no one seemed to feel the pain.

I had already accepted the fact that I wouldn't be returning to college in the autumn. The task of helping these wonderful people build the Heavenly Kingdom

**See* Glossary, page 143.

made all my previous ambitions seem quite meaningless. I realised that my parents would be disappointed. Noah Ross had warned us about this in yet another of his parables.

'A brother just like you,' said Noah, casting his eyes around the assembled brothers, 'goes home after a week at Camp K, anxious to tell his parents all about his experiences.

' "Dad, I've just had the greatest week of my life," he says, "and met all these wonderful people."

'But his father isn't listening. "Where have you been," he shouts. "I have all these wooden idols to make and you haven't been here to help me. You'll have to work twice as hard now to catch up."

' "That's what I want to tell you, Dad," says the brother. "I don't believe in idols any more. I've found God."

' "What God are you talking about," asks the father, looking around at all the idols, "the Sun God, the Moon God, the Horse God, the Frog God?"

' "No, I've found the real God," says the brother. "I want to go away and help him build the Heavenly Kingdom."

'At this the father beats the son. This doesn't mean that he is an evil man, only that he doesn't have the capacity to understand.'

This maker of wooden idols is supposed to symbolise all fathers, all parents who exist outside the Moonie orbit and thus pursue false goals. As Noah tells the story his voice changes, underlining the sincerity of the son, the bigotry of the father. It is more subtle than it sounds. Once the mind control has taken you over, you begin to associate yourself with the son; because there is an element of truth in this. If I had gone home to England and told my parents that I was giving up college to build the Heavenly Kingdom, they wouldn't have beaten me and they wouldn't have shouted at me. But equally surely they wouldn't have understood.

Towards the end of my first week at Camp Korea,

Bethie sidled up to me and whispered in my ear, 'We're going to give a party for God. Keep it a secret. He doesn't know.' Then I saw her whispering to the other sisters. I was worried that someone would speak too loudly and that God would hear.

Late in the day we took our guitars down to the main hall and crouched waiting in the darkness. Then Bethie switched on the lights and we all shouted in unison, 'Heavenly Father, this is your party. Heavenly Father, we love you.' We repeated this three times and with each chant we leapt three times into the air.

It seemed a perfectly normal thing to do.

Nine days had gone by since I'd first walked into Bush Street; and that's all the time they had needed to transform me to this.

I had the body of a mature woman and the mind of a child.

Chapter Three
DARK SIDE OF THE MOON

I am a thinker. I am your brain.' The Rev Sun Myung Moon

JENNIFER HAD the legs and the body of a showgirl and a face so lovely that it could turn over the heart of a man. Newcomers were always falling for Jennifer and it was hard to blame them. She was seated beside the lake at Camp A, another of the Unification Church's indoctrination centres situated at Aetna Springs near Santa Rosa, California. She was looking unusually serious, for she was about to embark upon one of the most important of all Moonie talks . . . the one which reveals in a roundabout way the identity of our mysterious Messiah.

'You must have wondered,' began Jennifer, 'how our community began. So today I'm going to tell you something about our founder, a man called the Reverend Sun Myung Moon.'

She paused, smiled. 'Maybe you have read about him. Some people call him Mr Moonie.'

But the faces all around her remained blank. The name had been introduced gently into lectures, but it had meant little to my companion and nothing at all to me. So Jennifer proceeded to tell us about this man who had been born in a North Korean fishing village on 6 January, 1920, the second of a struggling farmer's eight children. She explained that he had been arrested and tortured by the Communists simply because he had dared to preach a new gospel. So much blood had been drained from his body that he was pronounced dead; but three days later he rose again and continued to preach. Unable to silence Moon any other way, the commandant sentenced him to death. And this time he was saved by the arrival of the American troops under the command of General MacArthur who stormed the gates of Hungnam Prison only hours before his execution. In 1954 he formed the Tong-il Kyo or Holy Spirit Association for the Unification of World Christianity which is now known simply as the Unification Church.

'This poor man has suffered so much,' said Jennifer, tears running down her face, 'and he has suffered for us.'

By then many in the group were weeping. The Moonies live on such an emotional high that tears flow rather easily. Jennifer had been careful not to describe Moon as the Messiah, Lord of the Second Advent, Our Heavenly Father or The Master, the titles by which his fully fledged followers know him. The Moonies are coy about this during the period of indoctrination. They prefer to provide a series of clues and let the recruits find their own inevitable answer.

In the lectures we had been told that God sends a divine messenger to earth approximately every 1914 to 1927 years. First there was Moses, then Elijah, then Jesus. Jesus was born in AD 3 or 4; so this meant that the new Christ had been born somewhere between AD 1917 and 1930. We had also been told that like all true prophets he would come from the East.

Two weeks later I returned to the city, a fully fledged Moonie; and now every time I went into the prayer rooms, I saw the round smiling face of our founder ringed by gold and silver frames. We were shown numerous video recordings of his speeches. He spoke only in Korean which was translated by Colonel Peck, a former Korean army officer. I still hadn't realised the obvious; so desperate to learn the truth, I sought out Bethie.

'But who is he, Bethie,' I pleaded, 'surely you must know.'

Bethie smiled. 'To know the Messiah and to follow him is the most wonderful thing that can ever happen to you; but it's important that you discover this truth for yourself. However I can tell you this. You already have all the keys you need to supply the answer.'

'I have been thinking about nothing else for days, Bethie,' I said. 'Please help me.'

And Bethie who was never very good at saying "No" put her arm around me and said, 'Look at those keys once more. We know that he was born between 1917 and 1930. We know that in common with all of God's messengers he will have been persecuted and rejected.

'And we also know he came from the East. Now ask yourself this question. As he is a Christian which Eastern country would he be most likely to come from?'

'Korea,' I suggested somewhat hesitantly.

Bethie smiled and said nothing . . . and suddenly all the bits were fitting into place.

'Is it the Reverend Moon?' I asked. 'Is he our Messiah?'

Bethie had stopped smiling. 'Just go and pray and let God open your eyes.'

I went away, but there was really no need. I already knew. The reluctance of the Moonies to name the Messiah in these early stages is a safeguard. Moon's private life conflicts so strangely with his teachings that he has become vulnerable. If the man himself can be discredited so too clearly can the Church which is built around him.

On that day beside the lake Jennifer had warned us, 'People say terrible things about the Reverend Moon. Satan has put the words into their mouths.'

One of the most obvious conflicts concerns morality. Sex outside wedlock is considered Satanic by the Moonies. Any kind of friendship between brothers and sisters, however pure it may be, is discouraged. After you've been with the Church for three years, you may be 'matched' by Moon at a special ceremony. This means that he chooses your husband or your wife; and you can easily find yourself matched to someone you've never even spoken to before. You are permitted to reject the first two choices, but not the third. And then after a further three years, Moon 'blesses' you. This means that you are married; but you often have to wait another forty days before the marriage can be consummated.

A divorce within the Church is unthinkable.

Yet Moon has had at least three wives. Some claim that five is the true figure. Soon after leaving Vasoda University in Japan, he married Sun Kil Choi who has been described as 'decorative and not very intelligent'. He left her six months later.

He married Myung Hi Kim who majored in English at Yun Se Universiy. She bore him a son called Hi Sung Moon.

And in 1960 he married his present wife, the stunningly beautiful Hak Ja-Han. Moon was forty at the time; his bride seventeen.

Jennifer was one of the very few San Francisco Moonies who had been close to Moon. She had been a member of the New Hope Singers whom he looked upon as his personal choir. So I came to regard her as an authority upon the man I was now so anxious to worship.

I asked her, 'If Father is the Messiah, why didn't he marry the right woman in the first place?'

And Jennifer well versed in the answer had explained, 'God had prepared several women to fill the role of being the new Eve. But since they would all have to be raised out of imperfection to perfection by Father, there was a possibility that the woman could fail. After all it was Eve who failed in the beginning. Well Father's first wife failed. His mission could not be held back because of her, so God prepared our Mother for him.'

Much more damaging to the Church's credibility are the scandals which centred around its Messiah in his earlier days. On 22 February, 1949, North Korean police arrested Moon on a bigamy charge. He had married Myung Hi Kim while still married to his first wife Sun Kil Choi. He was jailed for three years.

On 4 July, 1955, he was arrested (this time by the South Koreans) on suspicion of irresponsible seruality· This came as the result of a scandal at the blue-stocking Ewha College where numerous girls and women lectuésrs were said to have become involved in the 'scandalous rites of the Unification Church'.

On 4 October, 1955, Moon was released, because the women concerned had refused to testify against him. They had exercised their legal right and remained silent in court.

Don Ranard, the former head of the American State Department Korean desk, has stated that, 'CIA files were full of sexual allegations against Moon.

'We were getting reports, calls and letters alleging that the Unification Church was a sexually orientated mixing of people in orgy-type fashion; and that Moon was the tester of virginity for new members.'

The Reverend Won Chei, a leading Presbyterian minister in Seoul, says, 'If we believe those who have gone into this group and come out, one has to receive Sun Myung Moon's blood to receive salvation. This blood is ordinarily received by three periods of sexual intercourse.'

Sa Hun Shin, dean of the religious department at Seoul University, believes that in the fifties Moon was practising the Pan Sexual Desire doctrine. 'This,' he says, 'is sometimes known as "the duty of the first night", a practice in which brides give their virginity to the chief of the region or to their priest.'

In 1963 a woman who had served as a deacon in the Unification Church came to the Reverend Shin for help.

'She was,' he says, 'in mortal fear. She told me that after witnessing Moon's sexual scenes she had withdrawn from the Church. But since then Moon's followers had made several attempts upon her life.'

Certainly his moral instructions to us were crystal clear. 'If a man tries to kiss you,' he said, 'bite off his tongue. You will be very famous. If a man is killed by biting, then at once the Unification Church will be famous all over the world. Afterwards no man will attack a sister of the Unification Church.'

Another instruction: 'Homosexuals must be changed. If need be, we will beat upon them.'

Time and distance have muted the effect of such scandals in America; and the Moonies dismiss them out of hand as stories conjured up by their enemies. They find it much more difficult to explain away the striking contrast between the Messiah's lifestyle and that of his followers.

While the flowersellers may work the streets for up to twenty hours in any given day, Moon lives in palatial splendour at his East Garden estate at Tarrytown just outside New York City. He is surrounded by servants and Oriental bodyguards, The grounds are protected by a patrol of black-belt karate experts with walkie-talkies. He has a fleet of cars including a custom-built Lincoln Continental, almost identical to the model used by the President of the United States. He has a powerboat even more spectacular that that of his neighbour Laurence Rockefeller. He is a multi-millionaire, possibly a billionaire. His business ventures are world-wide, ranging from real estate to fishing fleets, from gingseng tea to armaments. As he started out as a virtually penniless Korean, his rise might well have been hailed as living proof of the American Dream. Just one fact spoils the story. Seemingly from the very beginning this financial empire has been built upon the sacrifices of his followers.

In the Church's '120 Day Training Programme' there is an account of Moon's early days in Korea when he gathered his poverty-stricken, starving membership around him and directed them to give him all the money they had. He used that money to buy expensive clothes and instruments with which to start a girls' dancing team. The Training Programme recounts, 'People got angry with Father . . . He has no right. He is cruel. They must have felt this way. But Father didn't.'

Ten years later the dancing team toured America and were so popular that Moon was able to obtain an audience with President Eisenhower. The Training Programme suggests that this demonstrates his far-seeing wisdom.

He has been remarkably candid about his intentions. He once told his followers, 'I am a slave-driver to drive you out on a world mission.'

Another time he said, 'I am a thinker. I am your brain.'

And in 1973 he told his followers: 'Even in the Communistic army they are financially supported. They are given food, clothing, arms. But I am going to use you, trying to get money out of you. Are you ready to follow that kind of leader? You must be crazy people. I am sure you know that, if I am going to do that at all, I am not going to do that for my own sake. I have everything with me to support myself. I have earned quite a sum of money on which I can live all through my life. Some thirteen million dollars I have earned. With that, I can lead a well-to-do life. That money I have deposited in the bank, but I have bought land for you, to use in the future for international training centres to build and I have established factories to make more money for the movement. When I am telling you to make your own livelihood and even send some of the money to the Headquarters, I am not doing that for my sake. You well know that I am going to do that for the sake of saving the world.

'Even dictators like Hitler, when he utilised the people, he had to financially support them. Even Stalin had to financially support the people when he used them. But here I am, as the leader of this group, and I am going to use you by being paid! In that case I am the only example of that in the whole world in all human history.'

Moon once attempted to justify his affluent lifestyle in a speech to followers at Tarrytown by saying, 'In this rather materialistic country, I thought that we must have something to show. That is why I bought the estate. And in the future, when I invite to my home senators and congressmen and many VIPs from many nations, I feel I must show them other than the miserable side of life. That is also why I bought a luxurious car. Not for myself. In my everyday life, if possible, I choose not to ride in that luxurious car. When I do, I do it for the dignity of the Unification Church, and usually when I take my people with me.'

His political ambitions are boundless. They are also frightening, simply because his followers accept them so blindly. During my eight months as a Moonie, I never heard anyone question a single statement. Nor did I ever question one myself. Yet viewed in the cold light of day, they make strange reading coming as they do from a so-called Messiah of Peace.

Here are just some of the things he said to us:

'The whole world is in my hand and I will conquer and subjugate the world.'

'The time will come without my seeking it, that my words will almost serve as law. If I ask a certain thing, it will be done.'

'If the United States continues its corruption and we find among the senators and congressmen no one really usable for our purposes, we can make senators and congressmen out of our members.'

'We must have an automatic Theocracy to rule the world. The separation between religion and politics is what Satan likes the most.'

'Our strategy is to be united into one with ourselves and with that as the bullet, we can smash the whole world.'

'From this time, every people or every organisation that goes against the Unification Church will gradually come down, or drastically come down and die.'

'Let's say there are five hundred sons and daughters like you in each state; then we could control the government.'

'In case of war, we have to train ourselves for the rainy day . . . for the war to come.'

'Every one of you should have at least three spiritual children (converts) of your own who would be ready and willing to die with you.'

'Just imagine if America is monarchic and the President of America is like a king. If only he can understand Divine Principle (the Unification Bible), and if he can receive the Messiah and bow to him, then he has the absolute authority to cover all of the American people.'

The words may sound wild, even naïve, but it would

be wrong to view Moon as a political lightweight. He has been pictured smiling alongside too many American Presidents for that to ever be true. At various times he has shared the confidences of men such as Eisenhower, Kennedy, Nixon and Ford; and been an honoured guest at the White House.

Towards the close of 1973 and at the height of Watergate, 1,500 Moonies staged a demonstration in support of Nixon outside the White House. Their Messiah cried out, 'God must forgive the archangel Nixon . . . and bless America.' At this his followers immediately sank to their knees and began to pray.

He is motivated by a fierce hatred of Communism and an equally fierce fervour for South Korea. He was on friendly terms with the South Korean dictator and it has been suggested that the Colonel financed Moon's early American tours.

Donald Ranard has stated, 'No organisation as big as the Unification Church could have existed without some linkage to the Korean government. When the Korean CIA has infiltrated Christian churches in Korea to the extent it has, isn't it peculiar that an off-beat Korean church should advance so rapidly?'

According to the Fraser Investigation Committee, one of Moon's main business ventures, Tong-Il Industries is the chief arms supplier for South Korea; producing M-16 rifles, Vulcan anti-aircraft guns and M-79 grenade launchers.

At a conference in Seoul in June, 1975, the Church passed a resolution to establish an international corps of volunteers, prepared in case of war to defend South Korea 'to the death'.

If his dreams are grandiose, so too is the man. He was born as Yong Myung Moon which translates loosely into 'Shining Dragon Moon'. But he later changed this to the more God-like Sun Myung Moon . . . 'Shining Sun and Moon'.

On Easter Sunday, 1936, he had his first vision.

According to Moon, he was praying on a mountain top when Christ appeared before him silhouetted by the brightest light imaginable. A thunderous voice rumbled from the heavens, 'I am Jesus who came two thousand years ago. Now you will complete what I began but was unable to finish.'

Again according to Moon, Jesus embraced him as a brother. This was just the first of a series of visions which culminated with one in 1945 which proved to be the foundation of his ministry. We are told that Jesus bowed down to him and hailed him as master.

Moon's biography states: 'At that moment, he became the absolute victor of heaven and earth. The whole spirit world bowed down to him on that day of victory. The spirit world has already recognised him as the victor of the universe and the lord of creation.'

He began to gather his disciples and in the process he was excommunicated from the Presbyterian Church and also barred by the Korean National Council of Churches.

The Divine Principle was compiled with the help of Yee Hye Wen, a former medical student and a genius. His body was crippled, but his mind could soar to the most dazzling heights. In addition to a new bible, he also invented the revolutionary airgun which became one of the cornerstones of Moon's financial empire.

At the heart of Moon's theology is his interpretation of the 'Fall of Man'. He contends that Adam and Eve were born pure and intended to live in the Garden of Eden forever; but Satan seduced Eve and so tainted her blood. Eve then made things even worse by making love to Adam and bearing children. Thus their forebears, the entire human race, are 'fallen' and without hope. However hard they try, they can't shake off the power of Satan; because they are virtually his descendants.

According to the Divine Principle, God gave man another chance by sending Jesus. But Jesus failed him. Before he could marry and raise pure children, the purpose of his mission, he was crucified. Moon contends that this is why the Jews have suffered for almost two thousand years. They have been punished for failing to recognise the true Christ.

This is why the Unification Church now regards South Korea as the new Holy Land, being the spiritual home of its Messiah who has come to vanquish Satan and restore Heaven on Earth. The Moonies believe that it is their task to save the world, to help build the Heavenly Kingdom. It astonished me that the rest of the world were so slow to see this obvious truth.

When Moon said, 'No one can come to my depth of relationship with God. God is crazy for Father,' I accepted that without question.

And when he said, 'Master is greater than Jesus,' I believed that too.

Like my fellow Moonies, I felt that I was locked in a constant battle with Satan and the Spirit World. If I started to drowse towards the close of a long day, it was the fault of the Sleepy Spirits. If I began to feel unhappy, I was to blame; because I was allowing Satan to divert my thinking from Father.

In theory I was free to leave the Moonies at any given moment. I could have simply walked away. I would have been love bombed by my companions; but no one would have made any physical attempt to stop me. However I would have been stepping back into a Satanic world, abandoning all hope of salvation; and these are the bars which keep the Moonies in a prison of their own making.

I was convinced that there were evil spirits everywhere. I would sweep the floor over and over again and wash the shelves, because we'd been told that spirits often hide in the dust.

They were also said to be fond of the darkness, so sometimes the sisters would keep the lights on or sleep with an open copy of the Divine Principle lying across their heart.

I used to purify my food with Holy Salt. And if I had used up all my salt, I would blow on the food three times.

When I walked the streets of the city, I often carried a bag of Holy Salt in my pocket to protect me. One day a man became very angry when I was selling and threatened to punch me on the nose. When he wasn't looking, I sprinkled salt on his back to help drive away the spirits. Bethie told us that some of the spirits are very foolish. So when you purify a room, it is important to first open the doors and the windows. Otherwise these foolish spirits won't be able to find their own way out.

No one can ever be sure where Moon's acting ends and the reality begins; but there is reason to suppose that he does believe in Satan. In his Korean days, his followers would surround him when he travelled on a street-car to protect him from the spirits.

When he gives a talk, the karate chops are not intended to give emphasis to his words. They are warding off Satan.

Judith, one of the sisters at Bush Street, had been a servant at Moon's mansion in Pasadena. Before he arrived from New York everything had to be replaced, new carpets, new doormats, new everything. The floors were scrubbed for days on end. Even oranges and bananas had to be washed in case they harboured evil spirits. And the colours around him had to be white and gold, because these are holy colours.

Although she waited on him hand and foot, he never thanked, never spoke to her, never even looked at her. This didn't surprise her. She was just so proud to serve Father. It is only when you have left the Moonies that you come to realise what a cold man he is. But that very coldness serves to create the mystique which surrounds him. As a member of the cult I didn't regard him as a human being, just as a divine object of worship.

I could never understand why he made his speeches behind bulletproof glass. We had been told that bullets would just swerve around him; that when he went to the zoo, all the animals would wish to meet him; and that if he stood beside a pond, all the fish would swim towards him.

Every morning at five o'clock, I would attend a pledge service. There would be a picture of Moon to which I would bow three times, letting my forehead touch the ground. Then I would say:

'As the centre of the cosmos, I will fulfil our Father's will, and the responsibility given me for self-perfection. I will become a dutiful daughter and a child of goodness to attend our Father forever in the ideal world of creation by returning joy and glory to Him. This I pledge.

'I will take upon myself completely the will of God to give me the whole creation as my inheritance. He has given me his word, his personality, and his heart, and is reviving me who had died, making me one with him and his true child. To do this, our Father has persevered for six thousand years the sacrificial way of the cross. This I pledge.

'As a true daughter, I will follow our Father's pattern and charge bravely forward into the enemy camp until I have judged them completely with the weapons with which he has been defeating the enemy Satan for me throughout the course of history by sowing sweat for earth, tears for man, and blood for heaven as a servant but with a Father's heart in order to restore his children and the universe, lost to Satan. This I pledge.

'The individual, family, society, nation, world, and cosmos who are willing to attend our Father, the source of peace, happiness, freedom, and all ideals, will fulfil the ideal world of one heart in one body by restoring their original nature. To do this, I will become a true daughter returning joy and satisfaction to our Father, and as our Father's representative, I will transfer to the creation peace, happiness, freedom and all ideals in the world of the heart. This I pledge.

'I am proud of the one Sovereignty, proud of the one people, proud of the one land, proud of the one language and culture centred upon God, proud of becoming the child of the One True Parent, proud of the family who is to inherit one tradition, proud of being a labourer who is working to establish the one world of the heart.

'I will fight with my life. I will be responsible for accomplishing my duty and mission.

'This I, Sue Swatland, pledge and swear.'

Soon after joining the Moonies, I handed over my money, my traveller's cheques, even my credit cards. I may have given them to the movement; but in my heart I was giving them to Father. My only regret was that I didn't have more to give. One of the brothers had handed over a brand-new Mercedes and I envied him so much.

My spiritual father Eric, the rose-seller of Santa Barbara, had given me a picture of Moon which I carried in a pocket next to my heart.

I already loved this cold mysterious Messiah more than I had ever loved another man, or ever could again. I would have died for him gladly.

Later I was asked what would have happened if Moon had told me to kill my father, my mother or my brothers. Would I have obeyed him?

Even now I don't know what my answer would have been. I'm just glad he never asked.

Then there were the individual prayers. Everyone literally shrieked and the louder you shouted the more effective it was said to be. The first time you walk into the prayer room, it's terrifying. But after I'd been there a few weeks I became just as loud as everyone else.

Chapter Four

THE EMPTY ROOM

'Don't worry about us. We won't do anything stupid.'
Susan, postcard from Santa Barbara

ANNE

THE FIRST hint of trouble came with the morning mail. The letter from Sue was postmarked 'Berkeley, California', which meant that her schedule had been changed. This was Saturday, the sixth day of September and by now she had planned to be in Brockport just outside New York, her final port of call on the way home to England and a new college term. There was something odd about the letter too and not merely because she seemed to have lost all sense of urgency and time. Somehow it didn't sound like Sue. It could so easily have been written by a stranger, and this puzzled me.

How could I know that the daughter I'd loved for twenty years had already been brainwashed; that this was the standard Moonie 'Dear John' letter which thousands of parents have received over the years . . . the first of a string breaking the news that they have lost their sons and daughters, probably forever.

This is what it said:

> 'Dear Mum and Dad, Mark, Chris and Babba, (Babba is Sue's grandfather).
>
> Sorry I haven't written for a couple of weeks, but life has been all go! You won't believe it, but Di and I are still staying with the friends that I mentioned in my last card. It's been four weeks now since we met them, and every day since then has been absolutely fantastic.
>
> Perhaps I had better tell you a little about them, so that you can see that Di and I are in very caring, lovable hands. They call themselves "Project Volunteer" and are located in San Francisco, as well as

having a project in the country where I have been staying up until the beginning of this week.

It's a non-profit making project that was started by an American College Professor of English Literature and Philosophy. The people in the community are doing volunteer work, including international food distribution, property renovation, as well as being one hundred per cent concerned with human relations and general ecology. They are concerned with higher consciousness.

Since we've been here Di and I have done so many new activities; as well as helping out with the general housework and cooking, we've dug ditches, helped make walls (I can now mix cement quite efficiently), helped with the laundry, sewing, etc., etc. It's all such fun chipping in together.

It's amazing the type of people who are staying here . . . professors, doctors, engineers, teachers, scientists . . . all working together as one. I'm so happy here, and I'm gaining a new perspective on my life. Last week I was in the country, doing all the fun work that I mentioned above as well as swimming in the lakes, playing dodgeball and I've even had my first baseball game!

We also had lectures on human relationships and world ecology to help us understand the reason why there are so many problems in the world. Many of the people here are very intelligent and extremely interesting; and I have been deeply inspired by their idealism and good ideas.

This week in the city has been a little different. I've had a chance to put into practice everything that Project Volunteer stands for. On Monday we went to the warehouse where all the food and other donations are stored, ready for distribution. We spent the day sorting out sports shoes into their various types and sizes. Normally such a job might sound a little boring; but because of the people I am working with, all work is fun. Also since one of the local factories donated a lot of ice-cream in every break we're given ice-cream refreshments . . . in that one day, I had six ice-creams and two lollies. I'll have to jog faster!

For the last two days I've been out on the streets selling pictures. They're really nice, made in England and sent over here, framed and covered ready for selling. The money we get from them helps in the transportation of the food, also for petrol and telephone bills. It's interesting seeing how differently people receive you. Some flatly say "No", while others take an interest in what you're selling but don't have any money!! It's so rewarding when you make a sale, and each person buying a picture might be helping some poor person dying of starvation.

The other day we also went litter collecting down one of the main city streets. When people heard that we were actually doing the work without being paid, they were amazed. One elderly man even said to me, "If there were more people like you around, what a nice place the world would be," and another, "When I see people like you, it gives me hope in this world."

Well, as you can see, these people I'm staying with are the *best*. I don't yet know how long I'll be staying here, as each day seems so important and I'm gaining so much from the experience. Next week I'm going to stay in the city. I might go and work in the art gallery making the pictures we sell, or back to the warehouse to help pack food. It's so nice as you can choose the work you do.

I send this letter with all my love, and hope that all is well back home. I'm thinking of you all so much, and wish you were here with me.

Much love,

Susan

P.S. Mark, I hope the 'A' levels went well.

P.P.S. I'd love to hear from you all (the address is on the front).'

The address was: 1153 Bush Street, San Francisco, 94169, which meant nothing at all to me at the time.

I wrote back immediately to ask whether she intended coming home direct from San Francisco or would be moving on quickly to see friends at Brockport. But that uneasy feeling stayed with me, so I rang Di's parents. They had received a similar letter mentioning Project Volunteer and were equally puzzled.

I phoned the British Consul in San Francisco in the hope that he could tell me something about Project Volunteer. His voice at the other end was polished, polite; but as soon as I mentioned 1153 Bush Street, there was an uneasy pause.

'I am sorry to have to tell you,' he said, 'but this is the main town house of the Moonies.'

He sounded like a doctor gently breaking the news of some terminal disease; and I couldn't have been more stunned if he had. I told my husband Michael and saw my own shock mirrored in his eyes. Only parents who have been through the same experience can fully appreciate the emotions which threaten to overwhelm you at such a moment.

We didn't know much about the Moonies, didn't even know they were the Unification Church. However we did realise they were a really bad organisation and a newspaper headline came back to haunt us . . . THE CULT THAT BREAKS UP FAMILIES.

I had always believed that people who joined such cults were odd, even weird types; so found it hard to accept that Sue whom we knew to be a normal, intelligent human being could have become involved. Had she been secretly unhappy or worried about her life? I really didn't think so and yet there was still a feeling of guilt. Had we as a family failed her in some way?

Michael who tends to see a ray of hope on the darkest day pointed out, 'It's lucky you learnt the truth so soon. It gives us a chance to put things right.'

This was just the encouragement I needed. I knew that

for the sake of the family, I must somehow pull myself together, stay calm, never give up hope and do something positive to get Sue away from the evil influence of the Moonies.

Up until then our world had seemed so tranquil. Our boys, Mark and Chris, had settled down so well that the worries of parenthood appeared to lie behind us. We'd had a lovely holiday in France and now we were in the midst of an Indian Summer with the Kentish countryside full of bright reds and orange and yellows.

We'd had a card from Sue explaining that she and Diana had changed their minds and flown to Los Angeles, because the Miami flights were fully booked. We felt pleased as this meant they would be travelling up the west coast which sounds so much more interesting than the east.

Sue's happy-go-lucky nature came through clearly on the card. She intended having fun, to enjoy every single moment of her stay in America. The card finished with: 'Don't worry about us. We won't do anything silly.'

And now this!

There was a terrible temptation for Michael and myself to fly straight out to San Francisco, but sensed that this could be a foolish move. It was important to do our homework first, get some professional advice and find out what we were up against. So I contacted FAIR (Family Action, Information and Rescue) and they very kindly sent me a lot of information about the Unification Church. The more I read the worse the whole thing seemed. We were dealing with a throughly sinister organisation, ultimately concerned with power, even world domination. To read about the physical and mental damage suffered by the victims of the destructive cults was particularly upsetting.

We sent a telegram to Sue saying, 'Phone Home . . . Reverse Charges.' And soon afterwards she phoned. But was this really her? The voice sounded flat with very little expression, not at all like the Sue we knew. I pretended we didn't know she was with the Moonies and that we were still assuming she would be returning to college.

'When will you be coming back?' I asked. 'You'd better hurry as there isn't too much time.'

Sue hesitated so long that I wondered whether we'd been cut off and then she said, 'Have you received my second letter?'

I knew it was important to appear casual, so I said, 'No we haven't, but don't worry. You'll probably overtake it on the way over. Everyone wants to give you your twenty-first birthday presents, so hurry home.'

Sue's voice went even flatter. 'Wait until you get the letter and then we can talk again.' And with that, she was gone.

I already realised that the chances of her coming home were very slim, so the contents of that second letter didn't hurt quite so much as they might have done. It arrived at the end of September, having been posted two weeks after it had been written.

It was a very long typical Moonie letter, no mention of Moon or religion, but a lot about Project Volunteer. The crunch came on page six:

> 'I have to stay on here for a little longer, so that when I return I can love you all so much more, just like you deserve. I've thought about college so much, and consider happiness more important than a degree. If I want to go on with my degree, I think college will allow me to take a year off and then return for a final year. I'm in the process of writing. Anyway I can transfer to a college over here and get a degree that way. So if you're worried about my education, please don't be. I just feel that my happiness is more important at the moment, as unless you are happy life is not worth living. I can't over-state that I love you all . . . much more now since I've been here, as I've come to understand what was wrong with my attitudes to life. I ask

you from the depth of my heart don't think it's your fault. I think of you so much and it won't be too long before I'm home again. Just give me a chance to find myself and understand what life is all about.'

If all this had really been true, we would probably have accepted it and looked forward to having her home for the springtime. But it just doesn't happen that way with the Moonies. The weeks become months, the months become years, and all the while their ability to think for themselves is being eroded. Once they've been indoctrinated very few of them ever leave of their own free-will.

We had this terrible feeling of helplessness. Our daughter had been taken away from us by deceit, but there was seemingly nothing we could do about it. The police couldn't help, because technically no crime had been committed. Sue wasn't being held prisoner. She wasn't a minor and she was only too eager to state that she was already in the place where she most wished to be. Brainwashing and mind control were the crimes of a brave new world and the statute books had been slow to catch up. Freedom of religion was being stacked against freedom of thought. It posed an interesting point for intellectuals, but not for the parents.

For the first time in my life I needed sleeping pills and even they couldn't chase away the dreams. Every corner of the house conjured up some memory of Sue; but worst of all was her own room. There were the sundry trinkets she'd collected squirrel-fashion down the years . . . the souvenirs of summer holidays . . . and a photo album that traced the stages from tottering child to tomboy, from leggy hoyden to college girl. After a while I couldn't bear to go into that empty room any more.

FAIR had given me the phone number of Daphne Vane and I feel a real debt of gratitude for all the help she gave me. Being able to talk to someone so understanding just about saved my sanity. She stressed that it was essential to keep in contact with Sue, remain calm and stay on good terms. So as a family we made our plan of campaign.

We would write often and not allow ourselves to forget that the Moonies' mail is censored, sometimes withheld.

We would ignore the Moonie side to her letters and just reply to the Sue side as though dealing with a dual personality. But we always remembered that underneath she was still the same person we knew and loved.

We would use all senses when writing, talk about England, home, her friends and interests. We would constantly remind her of our love in the hope that she would realise that Moonies don't hold a monopoly on love.

We would talk to her on the phone at least once a week. Again we had to assume that calls were being monitored. So we would tell her about home and the safe subjects, get her to brighten up and then slip in questions. As soon as things became tense, we would change the subject.

I would press her gently but firmly on the importance of coming back to college. On one occasion Jacob came on the line. I suspect he had been standing beside her, listening all the while.

I said, 'Sue is letting so many people down by not returning.'

And sounding very Welsh from a distance of five thousand miles, Jacob replied, 'She is getting a far better education with us!'

A letter written on 25 September contained the first mention of Moon.

Sue wrote: 'Maybe you seem a little negative about what I'm involved in because of the name "Rev Moon". Well, it's true that this name can be attached to the community, but the word has become completely exploited by the media and turned into something bad. None of this is true. I'd have left if it was. After all I've had thousands of opportunities while in the city out selling on my own. But I've nothing to run away from.

One doesn't run away from happiness; from creating joy.'

She asked us to visit her in California so that we could see for ourselves. Her friends' families had been over, she said, and gone away feeling much happier. So Michael and I booked a flight for 22 October. I still nursed the faint hope that if only we could see her everything might still turn out all right.

Two days before the planned visit, Sue rang. She sounded dreadful, her voice really hard.

'Could you put your visit off for a while?' she asked. 'It's difficult at the moment.'

I told her we'd made all the arrangements and if anything her voice became harder still. 'Don't you understand,' she said. 'I'm saying I don't want to see you now.'

'Look, Sue,' I said, 'it's too late to change things. We'll see you on Wednesday and then we can talk together the way we always have.'

There was a long silence and then she said, 'I can't stop you coming, but it won't do any good. I won't be here.' At that, the line went dead.

I was terribly upset, because this was so unlike Sue. She had always been so considerate, so gentle with other people's feelings. I just couldn't imagine what had happened to bring about this sudden change. I felt it was more important than ever to go now, and Michael agreed.

So we made contact with Dennis Orme and the British Unification Church who guaranteed that:

1. We would be met at the airport.
2. We would see Sue alone.

I didn't really believe the English Moonies carried much weight in America; and so I still felt depressed. But the one thing I had discovered about my own black moods was that it's fatal to brood. Only action could chase them away.

With that thought in mind I hustled and bustled, preparing the evening meal. It was only some time later when I saw the wondering look on Michael's face that I realised what I'd done.

Caught up in the habit of the past twenty years, I had laid a place for Sue.

Chapter Five

THE DANCING DOCTOR

'If we help an old lady across the street, they'll say she didn't want to go.' Mose Durst, President of the Unification Church

THE CUSTOM-BUILT Mercedes stopped outside the Moonies' Georgian mansion in Hearst Street Two huge Korean bodyguards climbed out and surveyed the scene. Then satisfied that all was safe, they escorted Dr Mose Durst and his wife Onni up the steps of the mansion. Durst was looking very dapper in an expensive powder-blue suit with matching shoes, but it was his Korean wife who caught the eye. She was wearing a fabulous white fur coat which contrasted with her shoulder-length silky black hair and as she held up her hands, diamonds and rubies glittered under the lights.

They took off their shoes in the hall and donned golden slippers. As they walked into the lecture room, arm in arm, we all chorused, 'Oh, Onni and Abba, thank Heavenly Father for your goodness in guiding us.' Onni is Korean for Elder Sister; and Abba for Father.

They smiled and nodded in the manner of an emperor and empress; and in this company, that's what they were. Durst was the President of the Unification Church and perhaps a bit more besides. For now that the Reverend Moon had retreated to his Tarrytown mansion in Westchester County, Durst was beginning to emerge as the movement's new star. The Moonies, under fire from the media, wanted a fresh image and Durst, the amiable professor of English with his jokey Jewish ways, fitted that image rather well. It was Onni who had first seen the possibilities in this mild-mannered man. She charmed him, wooed him, married him and groomed him for power. And according to the Moonies who lived in the Dursts' Avalon mansion, it was still Onni who controlled him.

Mose (pronounced Mosa) is the son of Russian immigrants and grew up in the Williamsburg area of Brooklyn, New York. He is a graduate of the City University of New York and a graduate fellow of Cambridge University. And up until 1972, he was a professor of English at Laney College in Oakland, California . . . a lonely, disillusioned man who had just been divorced, retaining custody of his two sons, Tinker and Tim. That was the year when one of his students (a Moonie convert) invited him to dinner at the house of Onni Soo Lim, the supposed founder of the Unification Church on the West Coast. Onni was then at the peak of her beauty, a very exotic lady, and the college professor was seemingly overwhelmed. They were married two months later in a special Korean wedding ceremony performed by Moon. That break in the normal pattern of the Church is an indication of the importance of Onni and also of their plans for Durst. A professor was a considerable catch for the Moonies and his rise was rapid. He became state director of the Moonies in North California and then the Church's President.

It was an odd boardroom shuffle, because the Moonies already had a president named Neil Salonen who was very close to Moon. So one had to assume that the factions behind Durst were powerful ones indeed.

His plump face, bifocals and easy laugh gave him a fatherly look. He was a sentimental man, easily moved to tears, and much loved by the rank and file members. His college background gave him a certain kinship with many of the new recruits who had come from the campus. And he always seemed that bit more subject to human fraility than the other Moonie leaders. There was, for instance, his habit of raiding the kitchen for cookies in the early hours of the morning, a habit frowned upon in the Church. Any food taken before noon is said to encourage Satan. By some ill chance Durst always seemed to be bumping into somebody else also hunting for cookies in the dark. But there were never angry reproaches, only laughter.

He was fond of singing the songs of the Thirties and he would croon them in the style of a latter-day Bing Crosby. Sometimes on special occasions he would dance while a fiddler played and then he could look very Jewish, very amusing. The Divine Principle preaches the message that the Jews betrayed Jesus and this is why Korea has become the new Holy Land. And Moon has frequently been accused of being anti-semitic. But Durst made no attempt to hide his Jewish background. On the contrary, he sprinkled his conversation with Yiddish. Somebody would be *meshuga* (crazy), somebody else *schlemiel* (a jerk) and most of his jokes were Jewish too. He was an easy man to like and the media soon discovered that too. He handled them with a smooth, relaxed, professional expertise that paid dividends.

'Hey,' he said to one reporter, 'we're just like the rest of the crowd. We don't eat babies and sleep on nails.'

When asked about the Moonies' dream of a perfect world, he said, 'It won't be all that much different to the one we have now.

'The sun will still rise in the morning and set in the evening. It will still be a place where the Yankees can win the pennant and Reggie Jackson can hit home runs. But it will be a world of greater tolerance, self-respect and greater spirit of love guiding personal relationships.'

Pressed on the thorny subject of the Moonies' business empire, he shrugged. 'If you want to hold up standards, let's hold them up across the board. There is a church in America that makes approximately a billion dollars a year just through bingo games.' He didn't say so, but he meant the Catholics.

Asked why the movement had generated so much hate, he held out his palms. 'Maybe it's because we're the new kids on the block. I really don't know. You tell me. I just don't understand it. To know us is to love us.' He paused, smiled his gentle fatherly smile and said, 'If we help an old lady across the street, they'll say she didn't want to go.'

It was all good stuff and so often reporters who had

come with a hatchet job in mind went away wondering whether they had perhaps been wrong after all.

No one was more aware of Durst's good public image than Onni. She would tell her recruiting teams, 'When you go out and witness (recruit), witness to the people for Dr Durst. They respect Ph.D bag. But when people come into Family to stay, then you witness for Onni.'

But despite the sweetness, despite the sentimentality, the good professor had a very sinister side to his nature. He hadn't only taught English at college. He had a Ph.D in psychology too and had become an expert in mind control. The indoctrination methods used in the Californian camps of the Moonies are more effective, more far-reaching and consequently more harmful than those used by the cult in any other part of the Western World. Project Volunteer, the smokescreen which led me, and thousands like me, astray was his brainchild.

His personal lifestyle has become almost as extravagant as that of Moon himself. His Avalon estate known as The Gardens has seven bedrooms, a four-car garage, sauna, pool, cabana, a superb view over San Francisco bay and the kind of luxurious Oriental furnishings that only the very rich could even dream about. His cars are Lincolns and Mercedes, the carriages of the Moonie upper-echelon.

One of my favourite people Joe Alexander once saw Durst with Onni, the Moons and the Salonens in a Las Vegas casino. Joe had a former Moonie named Jeff Scales with him at the time; and Jeff like so many of us had really loved Mose Durst. Now he just stood there unable for a moment to believe the evidence of his own eyes. Joe, an opportunist, asked a girl photographer to take a picture of the group. Unfortunately the girl attempted to get Moon's permission and was angrily waved away. A few minutes later the Messiah and his party made a hasty exit.

Durst's small sons from his previous marriage, Tinker

and Tim, were staying at Aetna Springs while I was there; and they were two lonely little fellows. Onni considered them so fallen, so Satanic, that she couldn't bear to touch them. I have always loved children and so I used to spend as much time as I could with them; but this wasn't encouraged. Being Abba's sons, they were supposed to be segregated from the rank and file. Tinker, the youngest, had broken his arm and used to spend much of the day playing with the camp dogs. He was always asking for his father, but Durst rarely had the time to make those boyhood wishes come true.

And yet this seemingly kindly man had oceans of time for us his followers. He knew the names and the faces of us all; and on that day at Hearst Street as he walked slowly down the aisle, his head was turning constantly. He looked into my eyes and smiled as he went by. And this was part of his secret. He made each and every one of us feel very special.

We had prepared lots of little delicacies for Onni and Abba, a variety of home-made sweets, biscuits, little cakes and ginseng tea.

Durst, in a mock aside, warned, 'You mustn't tempt Onni too much. She's watching her weight.' He paused, gave a rueful grin and said, 'I think I'll be in trouble when I get home tonight.'

He glanced towards his wife, realised she wasn't amused and hastily changed the subject.

His talk, like all his talks, was a mixture of everything we had heard before, but laced with Jewish jokes and high good humour. When he'd finished he sang 'Only For You' which we knew to be one of his favourite songs. He sang it in the manner of a poor man's Frank Sinatra; and all the sisters clutched their hearts, sighed and even squealed just like the bobbysoxers we'd seen in the old newsreels. He was so delighted that he thought of doing an encore, then changed his mind and it wasn't hard to see the reason why.

Onni's face was set like stone.

Chapter Six

THE HOUSE OF NOAH

'*I guess somebody up there likes you.*' Neil Maxwell, counsellor for parents who have children in the cults

NOAH ROSS was sitting behind his desk, no longer the smiling, spring-heeled athlete. Even the voice had changed.

'Tell your parents they can't come,' he said flatly.

'But Noah,' I said, 'they've booked the flight, paid for the tickets.'

He shrugged in the manner of a long-suffering adult dealing with a child. 'Ring them up. Make some excuse. Be firm. They'll understand.'

I was still desperate. 'But they haven't seen me since I came here. They'll be upset.'

Noah was so accustomed to absolute obedience that the surprise showed in his eyes. 'You are not spiritually strong enough to see them,' he said. 'Maybe later you will be.' He paused and looked at me sternly. 'Don't tell me that you can't make this one small sacrifice for Father.'

As he well knew, the point was unanswerable. I went to Bethie with my problem. 'What possible excuse can I make?' I asked. 'My poor parents. I know they won't understand.'

And Bethie who must have handled that same question a hundred times before smiled reassuringly. 'Tell them.' she said, 'that you are travelling around for the next few weeks. This will make them feel better about things, because they'll see it as a sign of freedom.'

So I made my call, anxious to have it over and done with. I decided to keep it so brief that there could be no time for argument. My mother sounded breathless and strange and then to my astonishment I realised what was happening. My mother was crying and I couldn't remember her ever crying before.

I replaced the receiver feeling like a monster. But I knew such thoughts came from Satan. I must wash them from my mind. So I was glad when Noah sent me to Camp K. In that cold and lonely place there would be little time for thinking and none at all for regrets. However I had only just slipped into my sleeping bag on the first night when a message came from Noah. He wanted me to return immediately to Bush Street. There was no explanation. I hastily gathered my belongings and clambered into the waiting van, shaking my head, trying to drive away the sleepy spirits.

In his younger days Noah had been cursed with a stutter, but now it only returned at times of stress. So when he greeted me early the following morning, with, 'Your parents are come-come-coming and you must go down to Los Angeles and meet-meet-meet them,' I realised that the pressures were mounting. With the Unification Church under fire from the media on both sides of the Atlantic, my parents had chosen a delicate moment to arrive.

The British Moonies, very conscious of this, had asked Noah to make sure that my parents were allowed to meet me. He had agreed, but taken all the standard precautions. One of the brothers, a Canadian named Johnny B, would be my companion and bodyguard. His instructions: to make sure that I was never alone with my parents for a single moment; and to keep me out of the clutches of the Moonies' most Satanic enemies, the deprogrammers.

'But be care-care-careful,' warned Noah. 'Don't forget that your parents are from the fall-fall-fallen world.'

Johnny B was a good-looking, clean-cut law student with a certain claim to fame. He had been kidnapped on the instructions of his parents, had escaped after two days and returned to the Moonies as a hero. This was one of the reasons why he had been chosen to guard me. He knew how they operated. On the flight down he was unusually serious. 'I loved my parents,' he said, 'and I believed I could trust them; but I was wrong. You probably love and trust your parents, but remember you could be wrong too.'

He gave me two stories about the Reverend Moon which he thought would impress my parents.

The first was about a banquet which Moon had staged for a coachload of senators at his mansion; but the coach was delayed and so the banquet had to be cancelled. When Moon's servants came bearing dishes of rich food, he turned them all away, refusing to eat without his guests. He asked for cheese and biscuits instead.

'You see,' said Johnny B, 'what a humble man he is.'

The second story concerned a gathering of 500 of the world's most famous scientists at the Boston-Sheraton Hotel in November, 1978. The conference was chaired by the atom bomb scientist and Nobel laureate Eugene Wigner. Other Nobel prize-winners were thick on the ground. At the close of the conference the scientists gave a standing ovation to their founder and patron, the Reverend Sun Myung Moon.

'Those great men loved Father,' said Johnny B. 'Tell your parents that and they will begin to realise all these terrible things in the papers are just Satanic lies.'

At the airport in Los Angeles we were joined by a local Moonie named Walter. We stowed our bags in the boot of his car to protect my cover story. Noah had told me to tell my parents that I had been working in Los Angeles and that there was thus no reason for them to fly on to San Francisco. This was to be our tactic throughout the entire visit. As far as possible we would meet them only at places of our choosing, thus cutting down the chances of a kidnap. But so much for the best-laid plans! Somehow we missed them and, after hours of watching and waiting, we gave up and flew back to San Francisco. At Bush Street, I was given a message. My mother had phoned to say that they had arrived and were staying at a hotel in Fisherman's Wharf. She had left the room number. So bothered, bewildered and very wary,

I went to meet them with Johnny B beside me. We checked the corridors to make sure that deprogrammers weren't lying in wait and I put my ear against the door.

If I'd heard a lot of voices inside that room, I would have fled. But I could hear nothing, just silence. So I knocked, the door opened immediately and my mother was standing there with the strangest look upon her face. There was a mixture of surprise, embarrassment and affection; and these I had expected to see. But there were shock and fear too; and these I didn't understand.

ANNE

We had come to San Francisco more in hope than expectation. So when we rang Bush Street and were told that Sue was in Los Angeles, the doubts came flooding in. Did this mean we wouldn't be allowed to even see her?

I phoned Neil Maxwell who advises and helps parents who have sons and daughters in the cults. We had spoken several times before and as always he sounded calm and reassuring. 'Don't worry,' he said. 'I'll come round to your hotel at eight o'clock tonight and we'll find a way.'

At eight o'clock precisely, there was a knock on the door. Only it wasn't Neil. It was Sue. And we were in trouble. The Moonies consider Neil to be really evil; and if he happened to walk in while Sue was there, I knew that would be the end of our hopes. She would be spirited out of the city and hidden in one of the camps until we had returned to England.

So I hugged her and, thinking quickly, I said, 'We've been stuck in this room too long and would love to go out for a stroll. Is there somewhere nearby where we can get a coffee and something to eat?'

Sue's companion, Johnny B, said he knew a quiet place on the Wharf; and they seemed just as anxious as us to leave the hotel. It was only when we were out on the street that I was able to relax and take a good long look at Sue. The change was staggering. Just three months earlier she had been a fun-loving tomboy, bubbling over with the joys of life. Now she was barely recognisable. If I had passed her on the street, I could so easily have walked on by and never known this was my daughter. Her eyes were glazed over, devoid of any expression and she appeared to be on the brink of exhaustion. Her clothes were shapeless and at least two sizes too large. She was wearing a long, straight blouse, old-fashioned skirt, hideous shoes and worst of all thick, orange-coloured tights.

I hadn't realised that this is yet another thing you lose when you join the Moonies. Your clothes! They all go into a communal bin. So when you want something to wear, you simply help yourself. It's just one more way of destroying a person's identity.

Michael was talking to Johnny B whom we both liked and every now and then he'd glance at Sue; and I could see the pain in his eyes. They had always been such pals and I think like a lot of fathers he found it difficult to come to terms with the fact that little girls grow into big girls, leave home, get married and have babies of their own. He knew we'd lose her eventually. He just didn't wish to lose her this way . . . to strangers by trickery.

We had coffee and ice-cream and Sue asked me, 'Did you know anything about the Unification Church before I came to America?'

'Very little,' I said.

'I'm so glad,' she said. 'You see, if you had known you'd have warned me and I wouldn't have joined.' She smiled, unaware that she was rubbing salt into my wounds.

To change the conversation, I asked Johnny B whether his parents came to visit him. 'They used to,' he said, 'but not any more. We still love each other and we still write, but they're not happy about me joining the Church.' He explained that the Moonies needed good lawyers and that this was why he spent all his spare time studying. He seemed such a fine boy that I couldn't understand how his parents could bear to leave him in the cult. I had no means of knowing that they'd attempted to have him deprogrammed, and failed.

I was suffering from jet-lag and wanted to go to bed; but I was worried about going back to the hotel. I suspected that Neil Maxwell would still be waiting. When we eventually returned it was almost midnight and there was a note in my room, saying that a package had been left at the reception desk.

Sue immediately offered to fetch it for me, but I said hastily, 'Don't worry. It's nothing important. Just tourist information. I'll pick it up in the morning.'

Sue and Johnny B were both looking at me strangely. They left a few minutes later. I collected the package and sure enough it was from Neil Maxwell. There were some papers and a note. He had waited for over two hours. I phoned to apologise and explain.

Soft laughter floated down the line. 'We were both lucky,' he said. 'I was held up in the traffic. Otherwise I would have been there right on time and there would have been hell to pay.' He paused. 'I guess somebody up there likes you.'

SUSAN

Up until the time I joined the Moonies, I had always been very open with my parents. There had been the fibs of childhood, doubtless some wild exaggerations and a few white lies. But as a family we had always prided ourselves upon being honest with one another. Now with a little help from my new-found friends I had become a major deceiver. And this was the way Friday, the second day of their visit, began. I had promised to spend the entire day with them. However Noah Ross who was taking a very personal interest told me to change those plans.

'Make some excuse,' he said. 'Tell them you have some work to do in the morning. Don't let them get too close to you.'

So obedient as a child I phoned and said, 'Sorry, Mum, but I have to go down to the warehouse. I'll call you later and we can meet for lunch.'

'But surely you could ask someone else to take your place,' suggested my mother and I could sense the disappointment in her voice. 'After all we've travelled five thousand miles to see you.'

'You don't understand,' I said. 'I'll be feeding the poor. That's so important.'

There was a long silence and then she asked, 'Aren't we important too? Remember, Sue we won't be here for ever. It's only a short trip.'

'Of course you're important to me,' I said quickly. 'I love you. You know I do.'

I hung up before she could say anything else. She was confusing me and I didn't want to be confused.

And then compounding the Heavenly Deception at which I was becoming so adept, I didn't go anywhere near the warehouse.

ANNE

Sue's early morning call underlined our impression of the night before. Our daughter had become a stranger, someone we no longer knew or understood.

'It's as though she no longer has a mind of her own,' said Michael sadly.

Every now and then a glimpse of the old Sue had shown through. So we still clung to the faint hope that if we could talk to her on her own we might be able to make her think a little. Much of that hope faded when she arrived late for lunch with a new escort called Steve. Johnny B was spending part of the day studying law in the library. Steve smiled when we were introduced, but the smile never reached his eyes. He was good-looking, neat and wholesome, yet cold and hard. He drove us to a restaurant on the other side of the city, and the lunch was a disaster. Whenever I asked Sue a question which caused her to falter, Steve would answer.

He left us briefly and then returned to say that his car had disappeared, which meant that we wouldn't be able to go shopping as we'd planned. It just didn't ring true. I had been watching Michael throughout the meal. He is by nature a very easy-going man, but he hates anything underhand and I could sense that he was growing angry.

Eventually he looked Steve straight in the eye and said, 'I have the feeling you're setting us up. Tell me I'm wrong.'

Steve shrugged in a puzzled sort of way. 'I don't know what you mean,' he said, but he kept his head down.

Sue suggested hastily that we should go instead to Ned's Loft, the Moonies' art gallery nearby; and without too much choice in the matter, we agreed.

A crowd of young people were busy framing pictures which were to be sold on the streets; and as they worked, they chanted. It was a bit eerie.

Sue introduced us and they all smiled brightly. 'So, you're Sue's parents,' they said. 'Lovely to see you. We all love Sue.'

Some of the smiles seemed almost trancelike and so many of the eyes were glazed just like Sue's eyes. But there could be no doubting their friendliness, their desire to love and be loved. The young Moonies are really nice people, idealistic and oh so vulnerable, and it's impossible not to be touched. It's only when you study the older ones that the charm begins to fade. The smiles get that plastic look and there is a calculating look in the eyes that doesn't have too much to do with the dream of a better world.

There was a vivid, dark-haired girl called Brenna Steinberg whom Sue introduced as 'my little friend Brenna'. She was the smallest and most vulnerable of them all, just like a child.

She shook our hands and said, 'You must be proud of Sue. She works so hard.'

Before our story had run its course we would have the most poignant memories of Brenna.

Steve who had been coming and going mysteriously now reappeared with the news that his car had been returned. He said a friend had borrowed it. So he drove us all to 1153 Bush Street which was more or less as I'd imagined it to be . . . a tall, red-brick building in a quiet road. I asked Steve whether people knew it was a church and he pointed triumphantly upwards. Very high on the wall in small black letters were the words 'Unification Church'. Eagles could have missed them.

In the hallway we were asked to remove our shoes and again everyone seemed so friendly. We were taken to a small room and given a Mexican meal, all vegetables and very hot. Sue explained that they couldn't afford meat. And every now and then Michael and I would be left alone almost as though by design.

Michael slowly closed an eye and I knew we were on the same wavelength. We were wondering whether the room had been bugged and whether we were being encouraged to betray ourselves. So by tacit agreement we talked only of trivial things. After the meal we were shown into a larger room where the entertainment was just beginning, mostly old-fashioned songs applauded wildly. And then the smiling Noah Ross appeared to make a very professional speech full of jokes which attracted more laughter than they deserved. He was smooth enough to make it all seem very casual; but he was studying his audience and I don't think he missed much. Several times he glanced towards us and I did my best to look interested, even enthusiastic, because that was the game we had come to play. I wasn't really paying close attention. I was far too conscious of the new recruits, most of whom were easy enough to spot. The boys because they had longer hair than the resident Moonies. The girls because of their make-up and more stylish clothes.

They were already being isolated from one another and flanked by the older members. They were shown slides of Boonville and invited to the farm for the weekend. And I so desperately wanted to warn them that they were in the town house of the Moonies; and that if they went to Boonville, many of them would never see their families again. But to have done so would have sealed Sue's fate. We would never have been allowed anywhere near her from that moment on. So I stayed silent; and knowing what I knew, it was heart-breaking.

We returned to our hotel with a very real sense of relief and then somewhere in the night I had a dream rough enough to banish sleep. Noah Ross was smiling at me. A gentle, friendly smile that slowly changed into one that was taunting and totally evil.

Chapter Seven
THE LONG GOODBYE

'Look out for the Mountain Man with the fuzz.' Harry, link man with the rescue squads

SUSAN

DURING MY first few weeks with the Moonies, I made a secret pact with myself. We were constantly being reminded that parents were part of the Fallen World and therefore couldn't be trusted. We were also told that too much love for our natural parents was a bad thing, because it didn't leave us with enough love for our True Parents, the Reverend Moon and his wife Hak Ja-Han. But just the same I wanted to continue loving and trusting my parents. I wanted to believe that mine would be more understanding than others . . . that they would come to realise the importance of my task in helping to build the Heavenly Kingdom on earth.

I cherished the hope that they would join the parents' group in England who are sympathetic to the Moonies. And by the time Saturday morning came around, I was beginning to feel optimistic. They had been to Bush Street, listened to Noah Ross and today they were coming to Camp K to hear some of the more advanced talks. It really did seem as though they were taking an interest. So I rang to say that Steve and I would be coming to collect them . . . and the line was engaged! Instantly my doubts returned. They didn't know anyone in America, so who could they be talking to? I didn't even consider the most logical explanation, namely that they were phoning home.

Steve was standing beside me, shaking his head, looking very worried. 'I don't like it,' he said. 'There's something very funny going on. You just can't trust parents. Satan gets to them all.'

He stood there for a moment deep in thought and then he said, 'I think the best thing to do is go straight to the hotel. They won't be expecting us for another hour. So if they are working with deprogrammers, they'll be thrown off balance.'

We took another brother called Dave with us and it was real James Bond stuff. Steve stayed outside a phone box. I scribbled the number on to a slip of paper and hid it in my sock; while Dave stood in the corridor trying to look casual and succeeding only in looking like a jumpy desperado.

Mum opened the door. Dad was in bed nursing a headache.

'We've come to collect you,' I said. 'We ought to be on our way to Camp K soon.'

My mother seemed mildly embarrassed. 'We've decided to hire a car,' she said.

'But what's the point?' I asked. 'Why don't you just come down with us? You'll only get lost on your own.'

She smiled. 'You know us, Sue. We like our independence. We'll enjoy touring around.'

I was beginning to feel cross. 'You'll never find the camp or if you do you'll be late for the lectures. And if you miss the first part, how can you hope to understand? The whole purpose of your visit will have been wasted.'

My poor long-suffering dad with his aching head was getting cross too. He sat up with an effort and I realised how pale he was. 'We didn't travel five thousand miles,' he said, 'to listen to lectures. We came to see you, our daughter, and so far we haven't had a moment alone with you. There has always been some stranger on your shoulder, butting into every conversation. Don't you think you owe us a little more than that?'

Before I could answer, my mother, the eternal peacmaker, took my arm. 'Come on,' she said, 'let's go and have some breakfast. I'm famished.' And as we went out of the door she whispered, 'Your dad's got a truly dreadful head.'

ANNE

Neil Maxwell had advised us to 'Get your own wheels,' so we hired a car in Mason Street. I watched with some horror as they stripped off the brown paper. It was brand-new and I was to be the driver. Michael had left his licence at home in England. I had never handled a left-hand drive car before and found it rather daunting on the busy streets of San Francisco. By the time we crept over the Golden Gate Bridge and were clear of the city, an hour had gone by. We were a sorry pair. I'd had very little sleep the night before, having reached a stage where even sleeping pills couldn't give me the rest I needed. And although Michael had taken his aspirins, the head still ached. Still as we headed north through the lovely Californian countryside our spirits lightened a little. We stopped for a late lunch, removed all the anti-Moonie literature from our luggage and ditched it in a rubbish bin. We considered it quite possible that the car would be searched.

An hour later we arrived at Camp K and it was even worse than we'd imagined. The camp is surrounded by a high fence; and the only way in and way out appeared to be over a long wooden bridge across a river. There was a guard house on the far side of the bridge manned by a husky young man. And there was another young man leaning over the rails strumming a guitar. He seemed to be a permanent fixture. I would have found it easier to believe in his musical ambitions if he had been a little smaller. He was a tough-looking customer. The guard phoned to announce our arrival and we were escorted into the camp. We had missed the first two lectures and the third (Noah Ross again) had just begun. We slipped into the back row and I knew Sue was angry. She so desperately wanted us to listen and pick up this message of a new messiah. But you didn't need to listen if you wished to understand. All you had to do was look around you and it amazed me that this bright-as-a-button daughter of mine couldn't see what was happening.

Most of the Moonies were on the borderline of exhaustion. Many were almost asleep and yet still managing to laugh and clap in the right places. There was a girl sitting just in front of us looking very upset. Two older Moonies sat on either side of her and they rubbed her back during the entire lecture. I suppose this is an example of love bombing. I found it quite nauseating. I longed for her to come out of the camp with us and felt so terribly sad about leaving her.

Steve had booked us into a nearby motel at Healdsburg and we didn't feel comfortable there either. The owner seemed almost too friendly, too anxious to talk, to draw us out. So we were very careful not to even mention Sue while he was around. And when we made our plans for the following day, we did so in the bathroom with the taps running. This doubtless sounds melodramatic, but this is the way you start to behave in a situation like that. You stop trusting strangers.

After breakfast on the Sunday we phoned our younger son Chris from a public phone box and told him there seemed little hope of persuading Sue to come home. He went very quiet and I knew that he missed her as much as anyone. They had been very close. So I said, 'Don't worry. We're going to have one last try today and if that doesn't work, we'll think of something else.'

Sue and Steve were waiting for us at Camp K and by now his smile seemed even colder. He must have been getting as fed up with seeing us as we were of seeing him. He drove us down to Aetna Springs (Camp A) in a Moonie car; and this was truly a beautiful place. It was once a smart hunting lodge and people would drink the mineral water from the springs. The camp was isolated and surrounded by spectacular landscapes. It would have been paradise if it hadn't been for the residents. These were the saddest Moonies of all. Many of them had reached the zombie state. They looked like zombies and they even walked like zombies.

Some seemed to have lost the ability to even smile and there was one particularly sad case named George whose mind had clearly gone. He just mumbled. I couldn't understand a word he said. And when we shook hands, his hand lay in mine, totally passive. It was very creepy. He was the odd-job man around the camp. I asked Sue what he had been doing before he joined the Moonies and was horrified when she said matter-of-factly, 'He was a college professor.'

But the majority were such pleasant people that you were conscious of the terrible waste. We took a great liking to a New Zealander called Kim who was renovating the golf course. He was very knowledgeable about the trees and the plants and such good company. Then Michael asked him what he was going to do with his life and it was as though he had pressed a button.

Kim's face changed completely. The eyes went blank and the words flowed out, tape-recorder fashion. He told us how he was going to save the world. On and on it went, real Moonie talk. And then when he'd finished, he suddenly switched back to the nice, easy-going young man he'd been before. It was quite frightening because you knew you were dealing wth some imbalance of the mind.

We soon discovered that it was a mistake to interrupt these people. Sometimes they would go right back to the beginning and start again. Often they would get cross.

Michael had been planning to draw Steve deep in conversation so that I could at least have a few moments alone with Sue; and for a while it seemed to be working.

I said, 'Why don't you come back to college, Sue, and finish your education. After that, you could always come back to San Francisco. No one could stop you. But at least you would have given yourself the chance to think.'

She looked at me with much the same expression that I had seen in Kim's eyes and I knew what the words would be, because I had heard them before.

'What I'm doing here is more important than college. I am making myself a better person. My happiness is more important than a degree.' I am sure a few thousand other Moonie mums have heard that little speech down the years.

She went on to tell me how Communism was infiltrating the colleges of the world. 'I'm worried about Mark,' she said. 'You mustn't let him fall into their hands.'

'Don't forget,' I told her, 'there are other organisations just as bad as the Communists.'

At this Steve turned to me and was quite rude, saying, 'You don't listen to Sue and you keep interrupting.'

We were standing on the edge of a disused swimming pool and while Steve was still talking I saw the anger on Michael's face. His hands were rising and I knew precisely what he planned to do. He was about to throw Steve into the pool and there was nothing I could do to stop him. And then with an almost superhuman effort, Michael regained control of his emotions. He lowered his hands and thrust them into his pockets as though to shackle them for the moment. I don't know how much of this Steve had seen. But he moved warily away from Michael and away from the pool edge.

Sue looked so tired that I wondered whether she'd had any sleep at all; and she seemed glad when we decided to leave Aetna Springs. As we walked towards the car she let the distance between the men and ourselves widen, for once anxious to be alone with me. And when the question came, she was surprisingly direct.

'Have you been in touch with deprogrammers?' she asked.

I said, 'What do you mean by deprogrammers? We don't have them in England.'

She shuddered visibly. 'They capture you, tie you up and torture you.'

I put my hand on her shoulder and gave it a squeeze. 'How can you possibly believe that we could do that to you, loving you as we do?'

Her eyes dropped and she said very quietly, 'No, I don't believe you could.'

We said goodbye to Sue that night beside the wooden bridge at Camp K; and although the light was fading, we weren't alone. In addition to Steve, there were two men standing just a few yards away on the bridge watching our every move. They had parked their car beside ours and I think they were half-expecting us to grab Sue and make a run for it. I have good reason to believe that the Moonies hoped our visit to San Francisco would end in one of two ways . . . and that each of those ways would serve their purpose just as well.

Either we would come to the conclusion that the Unification Church was a thoroughly worthy organisation and perhaps even wish to join. Parents have fallen into just such a trap. Or failing that, we would do something rash and foolish, maybe have a terrible row or even better (from their point of view) try to snatch her and fail. They could then convince her that we were truly Satanic.

But we had been too well briefed to make that kind of mistake. We were there to build bridges, to see whether there was a chance that reason could still prevail. We drove back to San Francisco feeling very depressed. We had both accepted the impossibility of breaking through to the old Sue. She had been programmed all too well. And we were equally definite on another point. We weren't going to leave her there, abandoned in some faraway city, the deluded victim of truly evil men. Somehow we would get her out. It isn't until you feel you're losing someone that you realise just how much they mean to you.

So knowing that we had to be very positive, we phoned up an ex-Moonie and explained that we would go to any lengths to rescue her. We were given the phone number of a contact who would help. Even so I had a bad night and a bad day ahead of me. For early on Monday morning Sue rang to say she couldn't see us after all. She was going to the warehouse to feed the poor. This was to be our last day, so you can imagine how I felt. I knew she was acting under the orders of Noah Ross, but it still hurt.

So I asked her to have lunch with us in the hotel and

she hesitated. 'We haven't got a car today,' she said, 'so why don't you come round to Bush Street and we can have lunch there.'

'No,' I said firmly, 'just jump in a cab and we'll pay.'

We phoned up our contact whose name was Harry and he sounded very Italian. He asked us to describe ourselves and then he said, 'Right, now this is what I want you to do. Come down to the pier at seven. Make sure you haven't got a tail. Then take a look at the shooting gallery. Don't worry. I'll find you.'

'But how do *we* recognise *you*?' asked Michael.

A deep chuckle came down the line. 'Just look out for the Mountain Man with the fuzz,' said Harry.

We went sightseeing and were back at the hotel in plenty of time for lunch. Michael waited upstairs in our room in case Sue phoned and I waited downstairs in the lobby.

I sat there and willed her to come. I waited over two hours, feeling more miserable by the minute, realising that she no longer had any will of her own. This was the most terrible moment of all, the moment when I finally had to accept the fact that we had lost her. I went to our room and started to cry and I just couldn't stop. I had never cried like that before, or since. I felt so bad that when the time came to meet our contact I just couldn't cope. So I stayed in the hotel and Michael set out on his own.

I rang Bush Street and left a message at the desk, saying that we were leaving next day. And half an hour later Sue phoned to suggest that we met at Bush Street in the morning.

Deliberately keeping it casual as though it was a matter of no great importance, I said, 'What happened to you at lunchtime? I waited a couple of hours.'

Sue paused. 'I thought we had agreed to meet here. I was waiting for you.' Her voice was flat, seemingly devoid of emotion.

When Michael returned he was smiling and it was the first time I'd seen him really happy since we'd come to

San Francisco. He had arrived at the shooting gallery, circled it a couple of times and then a very tall man with a beard and a mop of hair appeared alongside. 'Keep walking,' said this mountain man named Harry from the corner of his mouth. Some ten seconds later Harry said, 'It's all right, Bud, you're clean.' And when Michael looked a bit baffled, he added, 'I mean you haven't got a tail.' According to Michael, it's not so easy to find out whether you're being followed as it looks on television. At one time he got the impression that just about everyone on the street was dogging his footsteps. He asked Harry, 'How can you tell which are Moonies?' And Harry replied, 'By their short hair and odd socks.' But the important thing was that the deal had been made. There were men who would be willing to help us rescue our daughter. In the meantime we had to return to England and wait. Harry would let us know when all the arrangements had been completed. It was a very good ending to what up to then had been a very bad day.

We said our final good-byes to Sue at Bush Street and even now Steve was with her. But we were determined to part on good terms. We had bought her a rather special Bible that she had wanted, some clothes and a batch of letters from friends at home. I took a good long look, realising that it could be a long time before we saw her again. And if anything went wrong with the rescue, we might literally never see her again. So I kissed her goodbye and said, 'See you at Christmas.' I knew there was very little chance of that, but at least I had to try. We caught a cab and when we got to the end of the street, Sue was still there, standing on the street and waving.

SUSAN

I kissed my parents goodbye with very mixed feelings. One part of me was relieved to see them go. The other part wanted to cling tight. And it was only when their cab moved away that I was touched by the sense of loss.

I wished then that I could have found some way to explain why lunch in her hotel had been impossible. But how do you tell your mother that you were afraid, because you didn't trust her?

Once again the doubts were flooding in. Their mood seemed lighter than it had in the days gone by. Was this some sort of trick? Were they pretending to leave simply to throw me off my guard? Were they perhaps even at this moment talking to the deprogrammers?

To find out, I rang home the following day and was almost surprised when my mother picked up the phone. She sounded bright and cheerful.

She asked me whether I liked the clothes they'd given me. I said I did. I didn't tell her that I'd handed them to Rebecca. After all, they had come from the Fallen World.

Chapter Eight
THE DRAGON LADY

'*If you go away, you dangerous, because you know too much.*' Onni Soo Lim (Durst), spiritual commander of the Moonies in California

ONNI CAME sweeping into Hearst Street, head held high, unsmiling, eyes glinting fire.

'Quick, *pali-pali*. Come sit,' she barked.

Pali-pali is Korean for 'hurry' and we hastily obeyed. When Onni was in this mood, tremors ran through the ranks. Our spiritual lives, which to us were everything, depended upon pleasing her.

She stood in front of us and those dark, fierce eyes slowly surveyed us all. 'Why you not sell more for Father?' she demanded. 'Why you shame me?'

Feet shuffled uncomfortably, but no word was spoken. We had been spending eighteen hours a day for the past few weeks, selling pictures, roses and candy on the streets, and returning each night with just enough strength to slide into our sleeping bags. During that time we had been bringing in around 150 dollars per person per day, but nothing seemingly could satisfy this handsome, forbidding Oriental lady. One of the newer sisters Judith was rash enough to point out that at this season of the year the city was quieter than it had been during the summer months. This only served to stoke the fires of Onni's fury.

'Bah,' she cried, 'you too selfish. That true reason. Stop your flirt with Satan.' She was interspersing her words with the karate chops that Moon uses in his speeches. She leant forward. 'You all work harder for Father. You make promise to me this moment.'

And with shame in our hearts we chorused, 'We promise to work harder for Heavenly Father.'

It would have been impossible to under-rate Onni's

position of power within the Unification Church. She was the female edition of Moon, fierce, fanatical and, with their Korean kinship, his favourite disciple. She was the spiritual commander of all the Moonie forces in California and bodyguard to Moon's wife, Hak Ja-Han, when she appeared in public. On matters of West Coast policy no one crossed swords with Onni . . . not even her husband Dr Mose Durst.

She was said to be so spiritually open that she could walk into a room and see the spirits all around her. She just needed to take one look at you and she'd know your spiritual state instantly, know whether you were closer to God or Satan. This terrified me so much that I didn't dare look into her eyes. We would scrub and sweep rooms for hours before Onni's arrival and open the windows wide, so that we could chase out the bad spirits. If we missed the slightest speck of dust or the minutest cobweb, she would be sure to spot it and rain down curses upon our heads.

This was one scary lady and made to seem even more sinister by the presence of her constant companion Teresa, an elder sister with mesmeric eyes. When Teresa became angry, which was often, even the strongest and bravest of the brothers stepped quietly around her.

Two prominent Californian Moonies, Jeff Scales and Evey Eden, had once been taken by their parents (under a court order) to the Freedom of Thought Foundation rehab centre in Tucson which was being run by the Alexanders, Joe and his wife Esther. Immediately Onni, Teresa and a band of their disciples set off in pursuit.

Upon arrival at the centre, Onni stood beside the front door intercom and barked repeatedly, 'Evey, Yacov (Jeff's Moonie name), my children, come out, come out.' Evey and Jeff were so terrified that they raced upstairs and hid under the bed. Evey's father, a lawyer from Detroit, asked Onni to leave and when she refused, the police were called.

She continued to scream and shout until a police car

arrived, then magically her mood changed, 'Why, sir,' she asked sweetly, 'wasn't I *invited*?'

Onni, Teresa and their followers were taken away in handcuffs and the Alexanders went in search of Evey and Jeff. They found them literally stuck under the bed and all four legs had to be lifted clear of the ground before they could be freed. Such was the terror that Onni could inspire. Is it any wonder that ex-Moonies refer to her as 'The Dragon Lady'?

At the subsequent court hearing some of the cultists were asked to confirm that they had no wish to return to the Unification Church. When one of them did so, Onni spat straight into his face.

On another day Mose Durst was halfway through a talk at Hearst Street when Onni jumped to her feet.

'Stop,' she cried. 'Sister fall asleep. Sleepy spirits get to her.'

And this poor girl had to stand up in front of us all. 'Come sit here,' commanded Onni. 'We chase evil spirit out. Smash Satan.'

The girl, looking absolutely terrified, was forced to sit at her feet. Durst continued with his talk as though nothing had happened at all. But every now and then his wife would aim karate chops at the air around the girl's head as though chasing away demons.

Onni had first joined the Unification Church in Korea and then moved on to Japan as a missionary. In the early seventies, Moon sent her to California to replace a Korean academic named Mr Choi (pronounced Chay) who had failed to make any impact in the state.

The Bay Area Moonies have an elaborate mythology wrapped around Onni's first two years in this new land. We were told that each day she would go to the Oakland Holy Ground and pray for God's help in building the Church. As she could only speak Korean, she was a stranger in a strange land, existing on four hours sleep a night and a starvation diet. Eventually God rewarded this self-sacrifice by providing her first disciple Kristina;

and upon this foundation, the Californian branch of the Moonies was built.

'How poor Onni suffered for us,' Teresa was fond of saying. I had heard those selfsame words from Jennifer; only in her case there was a difference. She was using them to describe the sufferings of our Messiah.

For such a dominant, hawklike lady, Onni could show surprising humility in the presence of Moon. When he came to stay at her Avalon house, she would reserve all the finest rooms for Moon and his considerable entourage. Her own room would always be the smallest of all.

Moon called her his 'daughter-in-spirit' and once in a jocular mood he said, 'I am a slave driver for God; but I think compared to Onni, I am a most gentle man.'

Certainly as a slave driver on the city streets, Onni can have had few peers. Her teams of flower sellers brought in the most money; her teams of restorers brought in the most new recruits. They were all motivated by the same potent ingredient. Fear of Onni!

Her advice on the best way to snare the innocents ran like this: 'Make friends, offer them whatever they are seeking, pray for Heavenly Father to guide them to dinner. Sisters get handsome men, brothers attract pretty girls. It's good if they come because they like you. Once in God's house, they learn to love God instead.'

Another bit of practical advice from Onni: 'When you talk to people, talk only about their needs, their benefits, find out what will get them in. In witnessing, if people get negative toward you, just say that we support all churches.'

She was quite definite too about the targets . . . college types, intelligent, good-looking, respectable, idealistic, healthy, lonely and ideally on holiday. They also had to be white.

'Black people don't fit in so well,' said Onni. 'Hard for them. Not right time in God's providence for them. Father says if whites don't accomplish then use blacks to shame whites in America, but not yet.'

There were no ethics on the streets. Heavenly Deception was encourged to run riot. One team from the Bay area, not mine, I'm glad to say, used to take out a van filled with wheelchairs. They would park the van in the early morning, climb into their wheelchairs and beg through the long day. Then late at night, they would put the wheelchairs back in the van and return to the centre with a fortune in donations.

Occasionally there would be rewards for the teams. They might be allowed to watch a rented movie such as *Lost Horizon*, *The Sound of Music* or *The Ten Commandments*. Or perhaps there would be a party with ice-cream at which Onni would perform the juggling acts she first learnt on the streets of Korea. Or if she really wished to show her gratitude to a sister she would take her to one of the multitude of massage parlours in San Francisco's Chinatown. But mostly we would give our eighteen hours of labour in return for a meagre starchy diet, the use of a floor on which to sleep and the knowledge that we were helping to build the Kingdom.

Onni's own rewards came on a grander scale. She would fly to New York just for a shopping spree. Her collection of jewellery was literally dazzling. And when her faithful disciples presented her with a beautiful blue Mercedes, her only comment was, 'Why that colour?'

None of the sisters, not even Teresa, could claim to truly understand Onni. Partly because we were in such awe of her. Partly because she was so neurotic, so unstable, so changeable of mood. She was convinced that her phone was tapped and that her life was in constant danger, hence the huge Koreans who guarded her on the special days.

But it was the Moonies who left the cult who created the true traumas for Onni. She didn't weep for them in the manner of Bethie the mother hen. No, Onni's motives were more practical.

'If you go away,' she said, 'you dangerous, because you know too much.'

Chapter Nine
BLUE CHRISTMAS

'*You are the Chosen One, Sue. God obviously has a special mission for you.*' Bethie

ANNE

I HAD always looked upon Christmas as the most magical time of the year. As a child I had been enchanted by the many mysteries; and as a mother I found it no less enchanting. Each year I had longed for it to arrive and been sorry when it had gone. But this Christmas was different. None of us could bear to celebrate without Sue. It's such a family occasion that she would have been the ghost at every party. We exchanged presents, but otherwise we behaved as though it was just another day.

To retain my sanity, I had tried very hard to blank Sue from my mind, but now suddenly it was impossible. Unbidden the memories came flooding back. I remembered a Christmas of long ago when I'd found Sue and her two brothers marching single file along the dark landing. The two-year-old Chris was in front followed by Mark, four, with the six-year-old Sue bringing up the rear. Mark and Sue were convinced that there were ghosts upon the landing and had persuaded Chris (who didn't even know the meaning of the word) to lead the line. The theory was that the ghosts, realising that Chris was unafraid, would step politely aside.

I remembered Sue the tomboy who in her pig-tail days had always wanted to climb trees and play football with the boys. She had once talked her five-year-old swain into inviting her to his birthday party. When I came to collect her I discovered that she was the only little girl in a room filled with little boys, a gatecrasher whom the mum hadn't had the heart to turn away.

And I also remembered Sue, the shoulderer of other

people's troubles, a girl who cared for the world around her; and as such, a girl who would be that little bit more vulnerable than most when surrounded by the love bombing of the Moonies. She had worked for a while in a home for handicapped children; and in her heart, they all became her children. She had loved each and every one of them. During a college vacation she had also worked as a waitress in an Eastbourne hotel; and got into trouble for listening too patiently to the tales of the more elderly residents.

I had nurtured wild hopes of rescuing her in time for Christmas; but I'd really known all along that this was too wild a dream to ever come true. So I kept in touch with our link-man Harry ('the Mountain Man with the fuzz' whom Michael had met that night upon the pier) and he constantly told me not to worry. Plans were being made, the rescue team set up; and as soon as the time was right he would let me know.

I also spoke on several occasions to the legendary Joe Alexander who would be masterminding the affair. From a distance of three thousand miles, he sounded steady, sure.

'No matter how long it takes, Mam,' he'd say, 'your daughter will be coming home.'

Michael was a great comfort to me. He behaved as though there were no doubts at all in his own mind. We would all have our happy ending. But I knew him too well to be completely taken in by that nonchalant front. He was working even harder than ever on the farm, driving himself to the brink of exhaustion at times. And every once in a while I would catch him with his guard down and see that tortured look in his eyes.

We had told Mark and Chris of our rescue plans and they were wonderful. They wrote regularly to Sue, keeping that oh-so-vital bridge in place and were touchingly attentive to my every need.

My father ('Babba' to the family) was constantly gentle and reassuring. But often at night I'd look across at his house, see the light still burning, and know that he was worrying too. He had always been very close to Sue and held a very special place in her affections.

We were discovering just how kind family and friends can be. Sue's college pals continued to write as though nothing unusual had happened. If goodwill could have solved the problem, the battle would have been already won.

I had packed my bag for the journey to come and placed it beside my bed . . . a constant reminder that it was only a matter of time before I'd be seeing her again.

SUSAN

A cold wind blew through the streets of San Francisco, lifting skirts and lifting hats; and beside me the lean Bethie shivered at its touch. But nothing could quench the fires that burnt within.

'God has waited six thousand years,' she said, 'for man to answer his call. We mustn't fail him now. You are the Chosen One, Sue. He obviously has a special mission for you.'

Bethie had always believed this since we'd first met at Boonville. She was convinced that God had directed my footsteps straight to her loving arms. Her faith was based on three happenings.

Firstly, Diana and I had come to California by chance. We had originally gone to Heathrow with every intention of flying to Miami. But upon discovering that there would be a delay of several days, we had flown to Los Angeles instead.

Secondly, we had gone to the Mexican restaurant in Santa Barbara on the very night when Eric arrived. This isn't normally a great recruiting area for the Moonies. But he was on a forty-day mission.

Thirdly, we had been given a lift and dropped at the very door of 1153 Bush Street. Few drivers are ever that obliging.

To Bethie, it was proof positive that I had been given a divine mission. 'You mustn't fail God now,' she said, putting her arm around me.

She always had this ability to make me feel very special. And if you believe, as I believed, that you really have been chosen by God, then everything else out there in the big, wide world pales into insignificance. I was there to help build the Heavenly Kingdom on earth and with that thought in mind no personal sacrifice seemed too great. The disciples of Jesus must surely have felt the same way.

This was why I was so amazed when I realised that Diana had chosen to return to the Satanic world. We had seen little of each other since our indoctrination in Camp Korea. So it took me a little time to realise that she had left. When I asked Bethie, she was unusually evasive. But I later learnt that Diana, almost on a whim, had packed her bag and walked away, oblivious to the pleas of the Moonies clustered around her.

I felt so sad for her. We had been told so many times that the ex-Moonies are considered the most Fallen of all God's creatures; and that for them there can be no hope of redemption. My aim was to work so hard for Father that I could pay off not only my own indemnity, but also that of my ancestors whose souls even now (according to the Unification Church) are in torment.

This was the faith and the fear that bound me to the Moonies far more securely than chains could ever have done. For me, a return to the outside world would have been a journey into terror. During my early days of actionising, I was riding into the city on a Moonie bus, eating ice-cream and having a great time. Then I looked out of the window at the people on the streets and it astonished me that I could have been so blind for so long. From my lofty perch, the whole world appeared to be Satanic. Our bus was full of happy faces; but there were no answering smiles out there on the pavements. The citizens looked grim and glum, filled with self-interest.

Some were smoking. Some were holding hands. Some were even kissing. They were really Fallen and it was our task to save them. I was so glad I'd seen the light and so anxious to spread it around.

But it wasn't easy to cast off the bad habits; and for most of us the hardest thing of all was to renounce the sensual thoughts. Lust was considered a major sin and only pure friendships were encouraged. In late October, I had begun to like one of the brothers, a fair-haired, husky, happy-go-lucky boy. We enjoyed each other's company. But soon we began to view one another with eyes that were not entirely fraternal. That's as far as it went. But that, by the standards of the Unification Church, was much too far. And it wasn't until I had spent many tearful sessions in the prayer room that I was finally forgiven.

Another boy admitted, head bowed in shame, that he had been feeling 'lusty thoughts' for me. Those were his words. So we both had to visit the prayer room. While he repented for those lusty thoughts, I repented for having tempted him. Was it any wonder that we were happy to wear the most unattractive clothing we could find?

Guilt was my constant companion. I felt guilty if my street-selling didn't bring in enough money for Father. I felt guilty if my spiritual children, the ones I had recruited, failed to stay. I even felt guilty if I became sick or unhappy. Because I had been told that these were all failures caused by my selfishness. I was giving too much love to myself, too little for Father.

Whenever one of my recruits returned to the outside world, I would pray for forgiveness. There was a boy called Thomas who had come to Boonville happily enough and then become very antagonistic towards me. He had fallen for one of the other sisters and my constant presence naturally cramped his style. He would shout at me to go away and leave him alone. And this was the one thing I couldn't do. One of the Moonies' golden rules is that new recruits must never be given the opportunity for free thought. Otherwise Satan will take over and their thinking will be negative.

Thomas became so frustrated by all this that he left and went back to the city. Dr John was furious with me. When I saw him the following morning back at the Trinity, he said, 'Have you repented?'

I told him that I had already spent an hour in the prayer room. 'Well continue to repent,' he said. 'You are a selfish sister. You have failed Father.' He was so angry that he was shouting. To a Moonie, such words are shattering.

It's only a matter of a few weeks before a recruit becomes a recruiter (in Moonie terminology, a 'restorer') and so the whole process is self-perpetuating. Although you are using deceit and downright trickery to lure people into the cult, you don't consider yourself wicked. On the contrary, you are locked in a constant battle with Satan in a bid to save all those poor people out there in the Fallen World. You are their only hope of salvation.

I seriously believed that God was putting people in my path and if I failed to lure them round to dinner, it was my fault. I wasn't being spiritual enough and God couldn't trust me with anyone's life. If they came to dinner and then walked away, I'd weep for them and they weren't crocodile tears. I felt so sorry for them.

We lived a very hard life in San Francisco, averaging little more than three hours sleep a night. Sometimes I would be so exhausted after the long day on the streets that it became a considerable effort to even climb the steps into the house. But no matter how tired I might be, I would still rise soon after four a.m. in readiness for the Pledge service at five. My body seemed to accept the fact that it would have to get by on a minimum of sleep and a minimum of protein. Our diet was essentially starch. But there were strange side effects. Girls stopped having periods. Boys stopped growing facial hair.

At times I was conscious of a sense of masochism. I

was wearing a spiritual hairshirt and delighting in its touch. I would suffer the abuse on the streets gladly, because this helped me to prove my love for Father. I was living on such a high that I seemed to be either in a state of ecstasy or despair, and nothing in between. It was so unlike any other experience that I've ever known. I was surrounded by a lot of love and for much of the time I was happy. But I also did more weeping than I had ever done before. They ranged from racking sobs which threatened to tear me apart to the silent tears of the night.

I sometimes felt homesick and longed for the warmth and comfort of my family. But Moon's teachings about such things were very clear. Parents in the Fallen World had never brought up their children the way they were supposed to; and so they had become the greatest barrier of all to spiritual salvation.

Even so when Christmas came around, my thoughts were constantly of home. This had always been such a happy time. I could picture Dad fixing the lights on the tree, Mum working away happily in the kitchen, Mark and Chris hiding their presents and Babba who in his own quiet way perhaps enjoyed it most of all. The Moonies don't really celebrate Christmas. It's not one of their holy days; so they make a token show, but nothing more.

For a moment I compared those two Christmases separated by an ocean; and wished that I could be home again, if only for the day. And then guilt came tiptoeing in. I began to pray.

Chapter Ten
BLACK LIGHTNING

'People don't realise you don't have to use torture any more. It's all done with love and kindness . . . and deception.'
Ted Patrick

TWO MOONIES had been kidnapped on the city streets within the space of a month; and the happenings had sent shock waves through the Church. Noah Ross's stutter had become more pronounced with each passing day. Onni was spitting words of fire at the two men she regarded as her arch enemies, deprogrammers Ted Patrick and Joe Alexander. Dr Durst had been moved to the brink of tears.

Rank and file Moonies such as I shared the outrage of our leaders and something else besides. Terror! Men such as Ted Patrick and Joe Alexander intervene only at the request of parents which presumably meant that Noah, Durst and Onni were safe enough. It was us, the more lowly brothers and sisters, who were the targets of tomorrow. We had been warned of the fate we could expect if we fell into the hands of these agents of Satan. A film had shown a brother being captured by huge and brutal long-haired men who had first tied him to a chair and then tortured him with sadistic glee.

The elder sisters had told us that the film was merely an edited version of what really happened at a deprogramming, because Dr Durst didn't wish to shock us. Pressed to reveal all, they made it clear that girls who resisted could expect to go through hell. Sometimes we would be confined to underground chambers, tied up and subjected to eardrum bursting noise. We could be stripped, beaten and humiliated, raped and tortured.

The elder sisters could afford to take a more detached attitude than us. It was a lot less likely to happen to them. If their parents had wished to get them out of the

Moonies, they would doubtless have done so by now. All of which may account for the harshness of their judgments. After a kidnapping, it was quite commonplace to hear one of the elder sisters say contemptuously 'She wouldn't have the guts to kill herself.' We had been programmed to believe in the principle of death before dishonour. Or to be more precise, 'If all else fails, physical death is preferable to spiritual death.'

Any brother or sister who escaped from the deprogrammers was assured of a hero's welcome by the Moonies; and much capital would be made of the story. There was one boy who claimed that Joe Alexander had suspended him upside down by his ankles and then poured a gallon of water down his nostrils. When I heard this, I had a mental picture of Joe. I saw him as a barrel-chested, sadistic thug. I could almost see the horns coming out of his head. Many months later I came to know him well. He is one of the kindest, gentlest and most sentimental men I've ever known.

I asked him what really happened to that boy and he smiled wryly. 'Whenever these poor kids get taken back,' he said, 'they come up with these wild stories. The wilder they are the more heroic they seem. But that was just about the daddy of them all. For a start I'm not even sure it would be physically possible to do such a thing; and even if it was, it would probably kill him.

'Put it another way. If debriefers such as myself really went in for torture as the Moonies claim, don't you think we could find something rather simpler? But all such stories fall down for the same reason. Whenever I debrief someone, a parent is always present; and what kind of parent would be party to that sort of nonsense?'

Joe gave me his version of the 'gallon down the nostrils' tale.

'The kid's former friend in the Moonies had been trying to talk to him for about twenty minutes. He didn't even look at her, just sat there staring vacantly into space. Finally growing desperate, she put a finger into a bowl of ice-water and flicked a couple of drops into the face of the boy.'

Joe shrugged. 'That's what you're up against,' he said, 'those poor kids have lost all touch with reality.'

He persuaded me to ring this girl and without any prompting she confirmed Joe's version word for word.

Another popular story has Ted Patrick chasing a naked girl across a lawn. Patrick is known as 'Black Lightning' in the cults; and for the obvious reasons. He happens to be black and he can move rather quickly. But like Joe Alexander he only carries out deprogramming at the request of the parents. So that story too would seem to have a flaw. Dads and mums don't normally encourage strangers to chase their daughters across lawns, naked or otherwise.

One day a girl who had been deprogrammed arrived at an airport with her rescuers. They were dismayed to find a small army of flowersellers from the Moonies and other cults operating in the lounge. So one of them put the following message over the tannoy: 'Will Ted Patrick please come to the reception desk.' Within seconds there wasn't a flowerseller to be seen. They had fled as though Satan himself was at their heels. And certainly I had always looked upon him as an ogre. That black face haunted so many of my dreams.

He is by any standards a remarkable man. He was raised in the red-light district of Chattanooga surrounded by areas known as Death Alley, Blue Goose Hollow and Murderer's Field.

'Death Alley was so bad,' he says, 'that the police wouldn't go down there, not even two-handed. You could kill another black man and you wouldn't go to jail.'

His father was a numbers racketeer and the family were desperately poor. He received only the most formal education, ran wild on the streets and suffered from a serious speech impediment. He worked on construction sites and as a truck driver. And from that unlikely background, he went on to the staff of the then Governor Reagan. He was appointed Special Assistant for Community Affairs in San Diego and Imperial County.

He might well have remained in that line of work for ever if the Children of God hadn't made what turned out to be a very serious error of judgment. They tried to recruit his young son Michael. It was 4 July in San Diego and when Michael failed to return from a fireworks party, Patrick organised search parties. Michael finally arrived in the early hours of the morning. He had a spaced-out look. He told his father that he had met a crowd of people with Bibles and guitars. 'Every time we tried to leave,' he said 'they grabbed me by the arms, made me look into their eyes. I never saw eyes like that before. It made me dizzy to look at them.'

Patrick didn't really believe the story. But during the following week, reports came into his office of other children who had gone missing on that selfsame night. In each case they had been traced to the camps of the Children of God. And if they were eighteen or over, it was apparently impossible for the parents to reclaim them.

Patrick decided to carry out his own investigation. He set himself up as a target. He went down on to the beach and let them pick him up. He spent four days in the cult and the event which maybe did more than anything else to determine his future came on the third day. A mother had come in the hope of taking her daughter home.

According to Patrick: 'The mother grabbed for her daughter, trying to drag her out of the house. But the Elders jumped her. One of them struck her in the mouth, two others pinned her arms behind her back, and they all fell to the floor. The woman was screaming and crying, the Children of God were roughing her up, and her daughter just stood there staring, without any expression at all on her face. They finally got hold of the woman's legs and arms and carried her to the car and told her to get the hell out.'

That night he dreamed of the cult leader Moses . . . David Berg. 'No doubt,' he says, 'hundreds of my fellow sufferers did too, but I'm sure my dream was a little different from theirs. I dreamed of seeing him behind bars.'

By the fourth day the mind control was beginning to get through to him. He knew that if he didn't escape then, he might never get away again. So he told them that he wanted to go back to the city, collect his car, his stereo, his musical instruments, his money and give it all to them. The lure was taken. He was driven into San Diego and promptly gave his companions the slip. Since then he has been engaged on a continual crusade against the cults. He has been arrested and convicted on numerous charges, including kidnapping and unlawful detention; and he has served time in New York, Pennsylvania, California and Colorado. His rescues can be rough and as a former boxer, he is formidable at close quarters. He is controversial and, according to opposing views, both saint and sinner.

He welcomes the publicity, because he feels that the great mass of people are still woefully ignorant about the dangers posed by the cults. He also welcomes the horror stories told about him by the Moonies and others.

'They tell their people,' he says, 'that if I ever show up, I'm going to rape them, beat them, drug them, lock them in closets, put ice down their backs, stuff chicken bones down their throats, deprive them of food and sleep. They don't realised that by so doing they're making my job easier. They come in scared to death of me, find that I don't do what I'm accused of, and suddenly they're wondering. Their minds are starting to work again and soon after that, it's all over.'

He is highly articulate and his words have done almost as much damage to the cults as his actions. Here are just a few of the things he's said:

'What I do is not kidnapping. What I do is rescuing. When I deprogram a person, he has already been unlawfully imprisoned. His mind has been unlawfully imprisoned by a cult.'

'The so-called experts on brainwashing make me glad I didn't go to college. Those people don't realise you don't have to use torture any more. It's all done with love and kindness . . . and deception.'

'Every one of the indoctrination cults has the capability of turning into another Manson family and, in fact, they're more dangerous than Manson, because Manson wasn't organised as they are.'

Although Patrick's original quarrel was with the Children of God, he now regards Sun Myung Moon as 'public enemy number one' as far as the cults are concerned.

'It doesn't take a rare genius,' he says, 'to wonder why a so-called Christian group would have to resort to deception and lying and the use of front organisations to recruit members. The conclusion should be obvious. Unless the Unification Church employed such methods, nobody in his right mind would join.

'There's just so much that a human mind can take. A lot of Moonies have died. Two fell down an elevator shaft at the New Yorker Hotel. Another committed suicide. There have been others who have been so fatigued that they have gotten in car wrecks. Then there are some cases where cult members have gone insane and killed each other. They have the capability of destroying themselves or someone else.'

Such words were never allowed to infiltrate Bush Street, Hearst Street or Washington Street. But even if they had, we would have dismissed them out-of-hand as the mouthings of Satan. Men such as Ted Patrick and Joe Alexander were considered to be the most evil, the most depraved creatures to walk the earth. We were terrified of their reputed brutality, but there was more to the fear than that. For these men were worse than robbers, worse than rapists, worse even than murders. They had been hired to take away our most precious possession of all, our immortal souls, our hopes of salvation.

As the cold winter lost its sting and the first buds of spring appeared, the rumours multiplied. We were told that new bands of deprogrammers were being recruited all over the city. A black man only needed to walk slowly down Bush Street and everyone would swear it was Black Lightning. The warnings of Dr Durst, Noah and Onni were constant. No one dared to be alone on the streets. Whenever possible we took a brother with us. We were wary, watchful and very worried.

Over and over again I prayed, 'Please Father keep me safe from harm. Don't let them take me away from you.'

Chapter Eleven
A MAN CALLED JOE

'*Until you are humble to admit the* possibility *that you might have been deceived, then you shall be deceived perpetually.*' Joe Alexander

ANNE

OAKLAND WAS spread out beneath us, dusk softening the landscape, the runway lights beginning to glitter. It was seven o'clock on the evening of 7 March, 1981, and the five long months of waiting were over. I had come in a bid to take my daughter home. But now that the moment was near, I found myself filled with mixed emotions. I was excited, but I was also tired (having been in transit for fifteen hours) and feeling very much alone. It would have been nice to have had Michael or one of the boys with me. I know they would have been good in a crisis. However this just hadn't been possible.

Mark was at college, Chris at boarding school; and as Sue made a point of ringing at least once a week, it was essential that one of us had to be there to answer the phone. Otherwise she would jump to the inevitable conclusion and be on her guard. If we had been rescuing a son, Michael would have gone. But in the case of a daughter, mothers are best and for a very sinister reason. Moonies are programmed to escape or failing that to commit suicide. So once they've been rescued, someone has to be with them at all times; and ideally this has to be mum. Luckily my cousin Lea was on a business trip in New York with her husband Bernard; so I did at least have one contact from home.

The legendary Joe Alexander had promised to meet me at the airport. We had spoken several times on the phone, but never met before. He said he would be wearing a blue-check leisure suit and as I'd seen him on television, I was confident that I would pick him out easily. And sure enough, as I walked across the tarmac, I spotted him near the terminal entrance.

He was looking towards me as though he wasn't quite sure. I said, 'Are you Joe Alexander?' and he stepped forward, smiled and shook my hand really warmly.

Had he been waiting long? 'A while,' he said. He shrugged casually as though it was a matter of no import. The plane was very late and my guess is that he must have been cooling his heels for the best part of a couple of hours. But Joe had too much style to say that. He was medium-sized, very tanned, fatherly, and his most striking feature were the eyes, dark, sparkling, full of fun. A reminder of his Italian heritage.

He introduced me to his companion, a big, tall, bronzed man called Dennis with the friendliest face imaginable. He took my hand gently in his huge paw and drawled, 'Glad to meet you, Mam.'

He wore jeans, a T-shirt and cowboy boots. He was an ex-Marine with long brown hair and a beard, and he really was a striking-looking man.

I had the feeling that I had seen him somewhere before and then I realised the truth. I had seen too many Westerns. Dennis was the good-guy sheriff who walks down Main Street, cleans up the town. At least he wouldn't have been miscast. As I was to discover he was a very good man to have on your side, in every sense of the word.

There are times when it feels good to be a woman and this was one of them. Joe and Dennis just took me over and all my worries were washed away. I was no longer tired. No longer alone. I felt wonderful.

Due to a baggage strike, I'd had a terrible struggle with my luggage in Los Angeles; taking it to another terminal and losing it twice in the process. Now these two picked up my cases as though they were weightless and suddenly everything was smooth and easy.

We drove away in a rented car and Joe said, 'We're

staying in a friend's house in the old part of San Francisco. I think you'll be happier there than you would be in a motel. From now on, you'll be with friends all the way. And when you finally go home to England, you'll have Sue beside you.'

The drive through the city brought back painful memories of my last visit and I was glad when we reached the house which was beautiful. It had wooden floors, dazzling white paint, high ceilings and archways filled with lovely green plants. It seemed to be full of people, all very friendly, all very anxious to reassure me.

Joe introduced me to another member of our team called Chris whom I liked instantly. He was quite tall, really good-looking with fair hair and a nice-sounding American voice. He was a former Moonie who had been rescued by his parents.

He said, 'This must all seem very strange to you. But don't worry. We'll get your daughter back.' He paused, smiled. 'This is one of the games that the good guys win.'

We had only reached our decision after a lot of soul searching. It's a horrible thought that you'll be using force against your own daughter. So I had been concerned about the type of men Joe would choose. I wondered how rough they'd be, whether it would be just another job to them or whether they'd care. Although I'd had glowing reports of Joe, he had still been a stranger right up to the moment we'd met at the airport. Now I knew I didn't need to worry about this aspect any more. Joe couldn't possibly have chosen better men. They were obviously strong; but as their attitude towards me showed, they also cared.

I was the only woman in the house and they'd given me a room with a mattress on the floor. The others were sleeping in the living rooms, the corridors, wherever there was space.

I awoke to find the room filled with sunlight. Spring had come early that year. There was birdsong on the roofs and that lovely fresh scent in the air.

As it was Sunday and we knew that Sue would be in

the country for the weekend, we spent a lazy day. We toured around gently just on the offchance that we might see her; but we'd have been surprised if we had. There were plenty of Moonies recruiting at Fisherman's Wharf and elsewhere; and just to be safe, I wore my hat and dark glasses. If I'd been recognised that would have been the end of all our hopes.

I spent the evening with Joe and the others in the house; and found it fascinating to just sit and listen. I'd heard so much about Joe that I was surprised to discover how quiet he is. His battalion had been in Normandy on D-Day and he had been in the first wave to hit Utah Beach. Later that same battalion lay claim to being the first Americans to cross the Rhine. But by then they had been decimated. Out of 900 men, less than fifty had survived.

'That kind of thing,' said Joe, 'gives you a new slant on life. It takes something real bad to make you ever worry about anything again.'

He first became involved with the cult ten years ago and quite by chance. It all began when his nephew disappeared.

This was the way Joe told me the story:

'My nephew was at college, a brilliant student and a fine boy, the kind of son any father would be proud of. Every weekend my brother would visit him and then one day he just wasn't there. He'd disappeared, no note, nothing. He was reported as a missing person and then six months later the police found him. He was living with the Jesus Freaks on a mountain just outside Los Angeles. My brother flew down to see him from Pennsylvania and was upset to discover that he couldn't even talk to his own son without the cult leader's permission. He left feeling there was nothing he could do to change the situation. So I went down there with Esther (Joe's wife) and got permission to take him to dinner. My nephew acted like a zombie, staring at us as though he was in some kind of trance. He ate as though he was starving. There was nothing left on his plate.

'I told him that his father was ill and needed him, but he didn't seem to care. He said that his father was only his "flesh parent". His "true parents" were the cult leaders. I couldn't believe what I was hearing. I said, "Look, your father loves you and you used to love him." He gave me that funny stare again and said, "Let the dead bury the dead." I figured he'd had a nervous breakdown and needed a psychiatrist.'

Eventually Joe and his brother took the boy to San Diego where he was deprogrammed by Ted Patrick. It took four days and then he suddenly stood up and shouted, 'Boy, have I been deceived.' He embraced his father and then called his mother in Pittsburgh, bursting into tears at the sound of her voice.

'It was the most moving experience of my life,' Joe told me. 'For days he had acted like he'd had a mental breakdown. There was a wall around him. And then with rest, food and reason, my nephew suddenly returned to normal. I can tell you, tears were shed all round that day.'

Joe had gone home thinking that this would be his first and last encounter with a cult. But a few weeks later Ted Patrick rang to ask for his help again; and soon rescuing victims from the cults became, for Joe, a way of life. Having come to know him, I can understand why. Like a lot of Italian-Americans, he believes in the sanctity of the family. It horrifies him to know that self-styled messiahs are deliberately breaking up families, turning sons against fathers, daughters against mothers.

He has been called 'the dean of deprogrammers' and he hates the phrase.

'It sounds so sinister,' he says. 'All we're trying to do is give these kids the chance to make up their own minds, to restore their freedom of thought.'

That term is apt, because Esther Alexander was director of the Freedom of Thought Foundation in Tucson, Arizona. After Joe had debriefed a cult member, she supplied love and a secure environment to prepare the ex-cultist for a return to the normal world.

He likes to tell the story of a policeman in Tucson who

asked to be present during the debriefing of a girl in the Moonies. Joe agreed on the condition that he wore mufti and remained silent throughout. The promise was made. During the debriefing Joe asked the girl what she would do if the Reverend Moon ordered her to kill her father.

And very clearly the girl replied, 'If Father asked me, I would kill my father, my mother, my brother and my sister.'

This was too much for the policeman. Forgetting his promise, he jumped to his feet and snapped, 'Young lady, if you repeated that out on the street, I would have you arrested.'

But my favourite Joe Alexander story concerned the rescue of a girl from Camp K. Her parents and boyfriend enlisted Joe's aid; and a remarkably simple plan was devised.

The boyfriend, a husky young man, simply draped the girl over his shoulder and sprinted across the bridge to a waiting car. Joe followed rather slowly in another car; and behind Joe, there were soon a long line of Moonie cars all trying to get by on that narrow, rutted road. Joe made that task impossible by stopping on a hump-backed bridge and studying his road map as though lost. By the time the Moonies had persuaded him to move on, the couple had disappeared over some distant horizon.

But life for the Alexanders has its more sombre moments. Joe was once ambushed at Chicago Airport by four large members of the Hare Krishna movement. They were planning to hustle him down into the basement car park But Joe, as befits a veteran of the Beaches, can look after himself rather well The police broke up the ensuing mêlée and Joe emerged unmarked.

Esther was also in the firing line. Her car had once been forced off the road by Moonies and rolled down an embankment. The Moonies, who must have realised there was a strong possibility that she would be either dead or dying, didn't bother to stop. Miraculously

Esther's car landed on its wheels in the dry river bed at the foot of the embankment with the engine still running. Bruised and shaken she drove back to the city and as she parked outside her house, the bottom of the car fell away.

She gets calls from the Moonies in the middle of the night. 'Next time you step out on the street,' warn the anonymous voices, 'you'll be one dead lady.' Many of the calls have centered upon her children with threats to chop off arms and legs. She has ignored them all which, in my book, makes her a very brave lady.

On that peaceful Sunday evening in San Francisco, we had no means of knowing that Joe and Esther were on the brink of one of their roughest-ever times; that the double rescue bid for Sue and her 'little friend' Brenna Steinberg would bring so much trouble.

We had been hoping that Sue would be back in the city on the Monday. When we'd last spoken to her she had been busy distributing leaflets advertising Durst's speech which was to be given on the Thursday. So we toured the streets. Some of us stayed in the cars, others walked the pavements with their CB Radios (walkie-talkies). They were very efficient and knew precisely what to do. The messages came back and forth over the radio. But at the end of the day, there was still no sign of Sue.

Then very early on Tuesday, Michael rang to say that he had just spoken to Sue. She was still at Boonville and likely to remain there for the rest of the week.

This was an unexpected blow, but we still checked the streets on the offchance that she might return. Just around lunchtime the police swooped on to one of our helpers, a young man called Danny. He had been sitting in a doorway (with the owner's permission) operating a walkie-talkie. The driver of a police car had spotted him and stopped. Danny had started to walk away, trying to look casual. But suddenly the area seemed to be full of policemen. They made him lean against the car while they frisked him. Then he was handcuffed and taken away to the nearest police station. We followed.

I walked up to the front desk and saw Danny looking very pale. He had been handcuffed to the rail. He was surrounded by some very big men, armed and tough. Danny had been very loyal to us, refusing to explain what he had been doing lurking in a doorway with a walkie-talkie. So the police had jumped to the conclusion that he was involved in an attempted robbery. They had called him a 'low-lifer' which had made him angry.

We decided to tell the truth. It was a gamble, but there seemed to be no other way. So I told the grizzled sergeant behind the desk that I was looking for my Moonie daughter and that Danny had been helping me. Some of the menace went away. The sergeant looked at me closely and then he said, 'Are you from England, Mam?'

I said I was and he nodded slowly. 'Take the cuffs off,' he drawled. He turned back to me and explained, 'We had no means of knowing.' His voice softened. 'I hope you find your daughter, Mam,' he said.

That evening back at the house some of the wilder, more adventurous spirits discussed ways by which Sue could be rescued from Boonville. With its high-wire fences and the creek which surrounds it, the farm is considered almost impenetrable. But an ex-Marine suggested that a couple of amphibious trucks could be driven through the creek easily enough on a commando-style raid.

Several agreed, but I could see the amused glint in Joe's eye. He winked at me and stayed silent.

Just before we went to bed, another key member of our team arrived at the house. This was Matthew, medium-sized, fair-haired, quietly-spoken and very deceptive. He was an ex-Marine, like Dennis, and had returned from Vietnam, disillusioned, and in that mood had been picked up by the Children of God. On one memorable occasion, he had tried to sell cult literature to Ted Patrick. 'I was with two other members of the Children of God,' he explained, 'and they were terrified. They retreated across the street. When I rejoined them, they said, "Didn't you know? That's Black Lightning." It didn't mean a thing to me at the time.' Because of those quiet, cultured ways, it was easy to imagine that Matthew would be more planner than man-of-action. But I never knew anyone calmer in a crisis.

We now had our team. Only Sue was missing.

Chapter Twelve

A PRAYER IS ANSWERED

'*You won't get Sue. She is far too smart.*' Brenna Steinberg

ANNE

THE DAY of Mose Durst's speech had dawned and Bush Street was a hive of activity. I had never seen the Moonies look smarter. The girls wore their very best skirts with the inevitable thick stockings. The boys had suits, freshly laundered shirts and ties. Their hair had been carefully brushed. The only incongruous touch was provided by the footwear. The rank and file Moonies were wearing training or tennis shoes. Only the cult leaders seemed to own proper shoes.

I was watching all this from a safe distance with Anne Steinberg, Brenna's mother. Misfortune had brought us together in a common kinship. But even without that link, I think we would have been friends. She was such a warm person.

With so many Moonies in the city, it had seemed a good day for hope. But we were becoming anxious as the hours drifted by, and all the faces we saw were the wrong faces By early afternoon they were beginning to move in small groups away from Bush Street and towards the theatre where the speech would be made.

Anne Steinberg turned to me, despair in her eyes and cried out, 'If there is truly a God in heaven, let me see Brenna.'

And incredibly at that very moment Brenna appeared on the street beside an angular young man in a green anorak. The message was picked up and the CB radio announced, 'Subject going up Bush towards Leavenworth.'

We held our breath and prayed, but we didn't have

long to wait. Within thirty seconds the boy in the green anorak came running back down the street. He ran as though he was being chased, his arms waving wildly in all directions. He seemed to be on the brink of madness.

He shouted something to another Moonie, then rushed into the house. Seconds later two boys came out of Bush Street in a terrible hurry, jumped into a van and took off on smoking tyres. It was a most incredible thing to see and reminded me very much of an ant's nest which has just been disturbed. Suddenly Moonies seemed to be running in all directions, but without any sense of reason. Panic had taken over.

Round about then the awaited flash came through on our walkie-talkie, 'Subject secure,' and for a moment Anne Steinberg looked stunned, scarcely daring to believe. Sometimes good news can be harder to accept than the bad. Then slowly her face was flooded with joy and it was a lovely thing to see.

I was delighted for the Steinbergs, Anne and her husband Morton; but I did wonder whether this maybe signalled the end of my own hopes. whether the Moonies would now be so much on their guard that a second rescue might be impossible.

Chris must have read my very open mind. For when we returned to the house, he said, 'You're quiet tonight.'

I told him why and he smiled, 'Look, it doesn't work like that. If anything it will help us. They may have spotted someone and been expecting something like this. But now Brenna's been picked up, they'll think it's all over. The very last thing they'll be expecting is another rescue so soon.'

He gave my shoulder a squeeze and said gently, 'Remember Joe made you a promise. He told you that you wouldn't be going home without Sue. Well, that's a promise we all intend to keep.'

Joe invited me to stay at Walnut Creek for the weekend and it was lovely with spring bursting out all over, leaves and blossoms on every tree. Almost the first person I met at the house was Brenna who was being escorted along the corridor. The men beside her seemed most relieved to see me, as her mother had slipped out. Brenna had wanted to take a shower and as it was considered dangerous to leave her alone for a single moment, it meant that someone had to go with her. They were only too happy to turn that task over to me.

Brenna seemed even smaller, even younger, even more childlike, than she had on the day I'd first seen her in Ned's Loft. As we reached the bathroom she looked at me in a puzzled sort of way and said, 'I know you, don't I? You're Sue's mum, aren't you?' Then clearly making up her own mind, she asked, 'Does she know you're here?'

'What do you think?' I said.

She pondered this for a moment. 'It's all right, you know,' she said brightly, 'I won't tell anyone. But I think you're wasting your time. You won't get Sue. She is far too smart.'

She was a nice little thing and I could understand why Sue was so fond of her; but that childlike air bothered me. The Steinbergs had told me that prior to going into the Moonies she had been mature for her years. I thought of poor George at Aetna Springs. It seemed as though Brenna's rescue had come just in time.

On the Saturday I had a message from my cousin Lea in New York. She had phoned Bush Street. They had told her that Sue was in the country, but that they were expecting her back in the city by Monday. They promised to leave a note on the pad, asking Sue to phone Lea at her hotel in New York. This was wonderful news and I suddenly felt much more hopeful.

Brenna was still quiet and unresponsive, but Joe didn't appear to have any worries. 'It's just a question of time,' he said. 'She'll soon start to think for herself again and then everything will be all right. But it can be a mistake to rush these things.'

On Sunday evening, Dennis drove me down to Bush

Street to see whether we could spot Sue. This is always the time when they return from the country. Several vans arrived and parked on both sides of the road. People stumbled out. They looked so exhausted that it scarcely seemed safe for them to cross the road. Then just after eleven a large coach stopped a little way down the road; and the Moonies who emerged appeared to be even more exhausted than the ones we'd seen earlier.

Suddenly I saw a girl with short curly hair and wearing a white coat. She looked like Sue, but I couldn't be sure. This girl didn't seem to be able to run properly and Sue had always moved like a gazelle.

She disappeared into the house and when she came out again there was a piece of paper in her hand. Could this be Lea's note? She ran back towards the coach, had a brief word with the driver and then sprinted up the street and jumped into a blue van. This time she was really running.

I told Dennis, 'I think it's Sue, but how can we make sure?'

He was watching the blue van closely. 'They'll be taking off in a minute,' he said, 'probably going to Washington Street. I'll get closer to her this time.'

We followed the van and sure enough that's where it went. They parked some distance from the Moonie house and remained inside. As we drove past, I pulled my hat down firmly and kept my face averted. We continued slowly round the block and when we came back they were still inside, slumped in their seats, seemingly too exhausted to get out.

We parked further down the road and waited. Eventually six of them emerged, crossed the street and started to walk down the pavement towards us. Dennis moved off very slowly and as we came alongside them, I took a really close look at the girl in the white coat. There were no more doubts. I was quite sure. This was Sue. It was a marvellous feeling. Beside me Dennis chuckled. 'A good way to end a day,' he said.

Dennis had been in a little-known cult, one of the most evil of them all, and this still astonishes me. For if you asked me to name a true Christian, I couldn't do better than name Dennis. He knew his Bible back to front, but that wasn't the point. He put it into practice in the most wonderful way.

We drove back to the house and told Matthew the news. He shrugged. 'We'll have a go in the morning,' he said. 'There's no sense in waiting. I'll give you a shake at four.' He sounded as calm as ever and I envied him that placid nature. I was far too excited to sleep; and due to our early start, I didn't dare take a sleeping pill.

I hadn't done much praying in my life, but I prayed that night.

Chapter Thirteen
THE PICK-UP

'*Subject turning right down Jones.*' CB Radio message from Matthew

ANNE

THE LIGHT of the new day came slowly. I know, because I watched it all the way. There was a red sky over the bay and I had no wish to think of omens. For now that the time had arrived I was scared, more so than I had ever been in my life before. It wasn't the thought of the Moonies that scared me and it wasn't the police. No, it was the knowledge that this was a case of now or never. In this kind of situation there are seldom second chances. If anything went wrong on the streets today, if we tried and failed, I would probably never see Sue again. The dream would be over. She would be given a new name and moved to some remote part of America.

On such a day it was comforting to have men such as Matthew, Chris and Dennis beside me. They seemed so relaxed, so confident, so anxious as always to reassure me. They introduced me to the newest member of our team, Mark, who was to be our driver. He was an ex-Moonie, pleasantly boyish, tall and slim with long hair and a beard. He was very intelligent, very thoughtful and I always had the impression he was searching for something.

After a quick breakfast we drove down to Washington Street in our dark-blue Ford with a large CB radio aerial on the rear wing. Dennis, Matthew and Chris were in the back and I sat beside Mark. We parked in a side street and I put on my dark glasses, pulled down my hat. Although it was still only four-thirty, the road was full of street cleaners, the most enormous black men with shovels and brooms. They looked really tough.

Chris turned to me with a twinkle in his eye. 'There has to be a better place,' he said.

Matthew strolled up the street to get a closer look and returned to report that Sue had left the house with five other Moonies and climbed into a van. She was wearing dark trousers and a white coat. The van had distinctive orange-coloured Canadian number plates. And as it drove away we followed at a safe distance on the quiet city streets. We parked well clear of Bush Street and Matthew left us again, this time taking his walkie-talkie radio with him. We waited in the car, keeping in contact. More than once we asked other users to stay off our channel, because we had urgent business. They were all very obliging. I was beginning to feel really tense as the minutes dragged by.

Then suddenly Matthew's voice came through, 'Subject turning right down Bush, wearing dark trousers and striped shirt.'

We acknowledged this call and started to move off towards Bush Street. The voice over the radio continued, 'Subject turning right down Jones.'

We sped down Bush Street, past the Moonie house and turned right into Jones. But there was no sign of Sue. She had apparently just stepped into a shop to buy some gum. Now speed was vital. We turned right up Sutter, circling the block as fast as we could. And this time as we returned to Jones, we spotted her instantly, walking ahead of us on the right-hand side of the street. She was with a girl in a blue anorak. They stopped to talk to someone near the corner.

Mark slid the car to a halt just behind them. There were no spaces, so we were double-parked. And it was at this point that I stopped watching.

I heard the doors open, then piercing screams, followed by a thud as Sue landed in the back of the car. I turned my head quickly and there she was, screaming, fighting like a wildcat, but Chris and Dennis held her fast. Her Moonie friend was also screaming and hanging on to the door as we started to move away.

The people on the pavement were standing, staring, momentarily off balance. One huge man was looking at me from just a few feet away. He was coiled, ready to spring.

I shouted, 'She's my daughter,' and it was as though everything was happening in slow motion. The tension gradually faded from that huge form and he stayed where he was. We were so near Bush Street that he probably understood.

Sue kept shouting, 'Help me. Help me,' and her friend was still screaming. It seemed an eternity before those screams faded into the distance.

Chris couldn't close the back door on my side, because Sue had locked her legs against it. I leant over and tried to help; and as I did so Sue gave me a really hard look. She had been so busy struggling that she hadn't yet realised who I was. I knew she must be feeling dreadful and once again I felt sad that it had to happen this way. But for such strong men, Dennis and Chris had been incredibly gentle. They had taken all the bruises. There were none on Sue.

'I'm sorry, Sue darling,' I said. 'We didn't want to take you by force, but in the end there was no other choice.'

The hard look stayed on her face, but at least she had stopped struggling. She sat upright between Chris and Dennis.

'I feel so sorry for you,' she said. 'You are going to be really hurt.' And then with genuine wonder in her voice, she added, 'How could you possibly get involved with such evil men?'

Dennis winked at me good-naturedly. He had clearly heard all this before.

I had expected the anger, even the hardness. But the thing that really surprised me was the fear. Sue had always been a dare-devil, a rough and tumble tomboy in her teens, certainly not a girl to frighten easily. Yet now she seemed to be in the grip of mortal terror. Her next words told me why.

'We've been told about deprogrammers,' she said. 'We've seen a film.'

Dennis and Chris were immediately interested and wanted to know what it showed. But Sue ignored them and continued speaking to me. 'They tie you up and torture you.' She paused. 'Mum,' she said, 'promise you'll stay with me at all times.'

'I'll never leave you,' I replied.

Her expression had softened just a little. 'I won't talk to these men,' she said. 'I will only talk to you,.'

She stayed silent during the rest of the journey. Mark had very sensibly kept well within the speed limits and although we had seen several police cars, none had shown any interest in us. He had glanced repeatedly at his rear-view mirror to see whether we were being followed. Then after a while he shrugged, 'We're clear,' he said, 'there's nothing on our tail.'

Even so it seemed logical that someone on Jones Street would have taken our number and passed it on to the police. We twice heard the wail of sirens, but both times they were clearly following someone else's trail. I felt some of the tension wash away as we crossed the Bay Bridge and began to leave the city behind us. A few miles later we pulled into a motel at Walnut Creek. We walked across the grass in a tight little group with Dennis and Chris keeping close to Sue. But she appeared quite calm, went inside peacefully enough and immediately asked for a glass of water. Dennis fetched one and she passed it to me.

'Will you take the first sip?' she said and her eyes shuttled between the two of us, watching for any re-action. I was amazed. Dennis and Chris were smiling.

Mark, who always seemed to be hungry, offered to get some food; and this seemed to raise everyone's spirits. Even Sue asked for a salad which was a good sign. Some Moonies have been known to fast when rescued.

For the first time that day I was able to take a good long look at Sue. The change in her, even since our October visit, was quite shattering. And it was no wonder I'd found it difficult to recognise her the previous evening. The eyes looked terrible and the face had become just another Moonie face. It was as though all the expressions I'd come to know and love over the years had been blown away. I knew she was my daughter and yet in so many ways she was still a stranger. It was weird, eerie, rather frightening.

The clothes made it seem even worse. They were truly awful and didn't even fit. I would have loved to put them in the nearest rubbish bin, given her some new ones and thus have chased away the Moonie Sue for ever. I only wished it could have been that simple.

I was still thinking about her clothes when a knock on the door startled me. I had already begun to feel like a fugitive.

Dennis slid back the catch and Matthew walked in. There hadn't been time to pick him up after Jones Street. We had been too anxious to get away. But it did feel good to see him. He made our team complete.

Sue seemed exhausted. She slipped between the sheets and immediately fell asleep. I wondered how long it was since she'd had a really good night's sleep. Or, for that matter, how long since she'd last slept in a bed.

I decided to walk down the road and phone Michael from a public call box. He was thrilled, but worried that Sue might still escape.

'She's very adventurous,' he warned, 'not the kind of girl to give in easily.'

I said, 'Don't worry. She's being well guarded all the time. These people really are experts. We couldn't possibly be in better hands.'

When I returned to the motel, Matthew said, 'We'll let Sue have a good sleep and then I think it would be wise to move on. I know a motel where we'll be safer.'

So in the early evening we drove to another town not very far away and another motel. Sue was escorted to her room, but again she seemed perfectly calm. It was quite spacious with two bedrooms, a sitting room, kitchen and dining room. The doors were locked, the telephone disconnected and with four able men around, I felt secure.

I went out with Dennis to buy some Kentucky fried chicken and assorted salads. And as he walked beside me in the darkness, he said, 'The most difficult bit is over. Now it's just a question of time. You can sleep sound tonight.'

After an enjoyable meal back in our rooms, they started to talk to Sue. Matthew told her exactly what had happened since the first day she'd joined the Moonies, how her mind had been taken over, how the truth had been distorted. He spoke very quietly, very simply.

And Sue just lay there trancelike, letting the words wash over her. But for the moment this didn't really seem to matter.

Later I lay in bed and considered the events of the past few days. First Brenna, now Sue. It appeared almost too good to be true.

Sadly it was.

Chapter Fourteen

THE MYSTERIOUS MATTEONI

'*Once I'm satisfied that your daughter wants to go home with her mother, I'll take them to the airport and kiss 'em both goodbye.*' Inspector Al Matteoni

SUSAN

I WAS awake, but my eyes were closed. Every now and then I would sneak a look at the picture of the Reverend Moon in the breast pocket of my shirt. For the first time in eight months I could stay in bed without any feeling of guilt, without the fear that Satan was getting to me through my body. I had explained to Heavenly Father that I was already planning my escape. But first I had to be strong; so I needed sleep and I needed food. I also needed to be fit; so I did my isometric exercises right through the day, even while lying in bed.

When Matthew and the others talked to me, I blanked off my mind. I prayed. I chanted. I conjured up the faces of everyone in Doctor John's Trinity. I'd look at my watch and know what they would all be doing at this given moment. It made it seem as though they were still with me. And I remained passive, anxious to lull them into a false sense of security.

My intentions were very simple. I would either escape or I would die. This was my duty. I had been told so a hundred times or more. I wasn't afraid of physical death, but I was terrified of spiritual death. And if I weakened and allowed myself to slip back into the hands of Satan, this would be my fate.

My best chance seemed to lie in crashing through the sitting-room window. There wouldn't be time to open it. I wasn't worried about the glass and I wasn't worried about the twenty-foot fall. I could hit the ground and roll. But I was worried about hitting the concrete and breaking a leg, because then I wouldn't be able to get away.

Still I felt that with a bit of help from Heavenly Father, I could succeed. Once out on the street, I would run against the oncoming traffic, waving until somebody stopped.

I had other ideas. There was a fencing foil in the room which I considered using as a weapon. But although these men were Satanic, I didn't really want to hurt them. Or I could ask my guard for a glass of water in the middle of the night. Hopefully he would let me fetch it and follow me to the bathroom. Then I could squirt liquid soap in his eyes and make a run for it. I thought it best to try this when Matthew was the guard. He was the smallest and I felt he'd be the easiest to fight. I didn't know he was an ex-Marine!

ANNE

It was marvellous to wake up and see Sue in the next bed. I had to pinch myself to make sure it was really true. She was still talking only to me. As soon as the others spoke, she would switch herself off. It must have been like talking to a brick wall. Terribly frustrating, but they remained calm, quiet and oh so patient. I felt sure she wouldn't be able to keep this up for ever, that eventually she would realise the truth. So I was beginning to feel good and it was then that the blow fell.

Matthew had left to phone our link man Harry. He returned looking unusually sombre and gestured at me to follow him into the next room.

'Bad news,' he said. 'The police have picked up Joe, three of the others and Brenna. Joe and his team are in jail charged with kidnapping, false imprisonment, and conspiracy to kidnap; and Brenna's back in the Moonies.'

'Does that mean there's no hope for Brenna?' I asked.

Matthew shrugged. 'It would take a miracle to ever

get her out again,' he said. He wasn't the kind to hand out false hope.

It was only later that I learnt the full story behind the arrest from those involved. The police, headed by Inspector Al Matteoni and Inspector Tom Arnold, had located Morton and Anne Steinberg at the Walnut Creek motel we had left only a few hours earlier. They had arrived shortly before three o'clock in the morning. Matteoni had asked the Steinbergs to take him to the place where Brenna was being held. At first they refused. But then according to their testimony, Matteoni had said, 'Look, I'm a family man myself. I know how you feel. All we want to do is see your daughter and ask a couple of questions. We just want to be reassured that she hasn't been physically abused and is now staying there of her own free-will. That's all. If she says that, we'll go away and leave you in peace. Now what could be fairer than that?'

By that stage Brenna had already been deprogrammed, but these were still very early days. Several weeks of rehabilitation are usually required before the mind is really thinking freely. After some soul-searching the Steinbergs finally agreed to lead the police to Brenna. She was still in the Walnut Creek house where I had spent the weekend. The door was opened by Joe Alexander who said that Brenna was sound asleep, but offered to wake her up.

At that point there was a dramatic change in the attitude of the police. The 'family man' mood of Matteoni was shed like a cloak. Joe and his three companions were handcuffed and told to 'keep their traps shut'. Matteoni burst into Brenna's room and shouted, 'Get up. You've been kidnapped.' Morton's request to speak to Brenna alone was ignored. She was hustled into the back seat of a police car. When poor Anne Steinberg tried to reach her, she was brushed aside. To her horror, she saw her daughter's face turning again into a Moonie face.

Brenna was taken to the police station and love

bombed by fellow Moonies. And that still very fragile mind snapped once more. She was returned to Bush Street. Anne and Morton had also been at the station; but, unlike the Moonies, were not allowed to see Brenna.

A report in the *San Francisco Chronicle* had this to say:

'Mose Durst, national president of the Unification Church, whose 30,000 devotees are followers of the Rev Sun Myung Moon, said Steinberg was beaten, insulted, cursed, kept awake and told her religious faith was "garbage" during her ordeal. Police, however, would not confirm reports that Steinberg was physically abused.

'Police are still looking for a friend of Steinberg's, Susan Swatland of Ashford, Kent, England, who was reportedly grabbed by three men who forced her into a car Monday morning as she was walking down the 800 block of Jones Street.

'Michael Swatland, Susan's father and a well-to-do chicken rancher, said Monday during a telephone interview from England, that his wife and daughter are in the Bay Area but would not reveal their whereabouts.

'Police believe Swatland's abduction is connected to the Steinberg kidnapping, and that Swatland may have been held for deprogramming at the same Walnut Creek residence.

'Both young women joined the Moonies last July and stayed at the Bush Street commune over their parents' strenuous objections, authorities said.

'Durst said there have been four Moonie kidnappings during the last three months in the Bay Area. One Church official said Church members 'are living in a state of fear and suspicion and are afraid to walk down the street.'

An interesting sidelight on all this came at the police station. Joe and his three companions were sitting on a bench waiting to be charged when a sergeant walked by.

'What are those guys doing there?' he asked.

A detective said, 'Those are the guys who snatched the Steinberg kid from the Moonies.'

'And we arrested them?' said the sergeant in disbelief. 'We should have pinned medals on them.'

Now that they'd found Brenna, the hunt for us was being intensified. They had visited our house in San Francisco, finding my luggage clearly labelled. They were checking all the hotels and motels around the city. And the police weren't the only ones. The Moonies' strong-arm squad was searching for us too.

Poor Esther Alexander, with her husband in jail, was again being threatened by the more violent members of the cult. Acid had been poured over the paintwork of her car. Moonies would press their faces against the windows of her house. And there would be anonymous calls in the dark of night.

Susan's picture was shown in the newspapers and on television. And our car number was given over the radio. By the time we heard about this, the car had been standing outside the motel and in full view of the road for hours. Without a word, Dennis climbed in and drove it away. As time passed we became very anxious. But eventually he returned with another car and came strolling into the motel, casual as you please.

'No problems?' asked Matthew.

Dennis shrugged those big shoulders. 'Easy as picking berries,' he said.

We were careful not to let Sue know we were worried. For if she discovered that the police and the Moonies were searching for us in such force, she might be encouraged to remain in that trancelike state for days.

And as Matthew stressed, 'We are in a race against time. We have to accept the possibility that the police may catch up with us. But before that happens, it's vital that we break through,.'

He didn't elaborate. There was no need. We all understood. Once Sue came to realise how she had been hoodwinked, the police would be powerless to intervene. They couldn't arrest us as kidnappers, because there would no longer be a victim. And much more important from my point of view, Sue wouldn't be returning into the Moonies. I had reached a stage when I no longer cared what happened to me. If I had to go to jail, so be it. This was a price I would gladly pay, just so long as it meant that Sue would be going home. There was nothing very noble about this or sacrificial. It was simply a question of options. If Sue had to continue existing (not living) in this most evil cult . . . if this destruction of a fine human being was to be continued . . . then there could be no hope of happiness for me. Once you've come to that point, all the normal worries of your world suddenly seem petty by comparison.

Matthew thought we would be safe for just one more day in our present motel, because the police were still concentrating their search in a circle around the city. His sixth-sense had saved us at Walnut Creek, so I accepted his judgment again without question. But just the same I had never felt so frightened in my life. Police cars kept going by on the main road and every time I heard the sirens, my heart beat a little faster. To add to my problems, I'd left my sleeping pills with my luggage in San Francisco. They would never be needed more.

Clearly sensing this, Chris took me for a sunlit walk on the Wednesday afternoon. He told me about his days in the Moonies and I was touched by the lack of bitterness.

'The great bonus,' he said, 'was that I met some of the nicest people I've ever known. There were all these young guys and girls with such fine ideals and so much love for their fellow humans.'

He paused. 'That's the real crime,' he said. 'The one unforgivable sin, that so much goodness should be exploited by a small band of evil men.'

His own rescue from the cult had been a dramatic one. He had been seized by three big men and dragged into the back of a car. I can only imagine that they must have been very big men indeed! One of his fellow Moonies had advanced armed with a baseball bat.

'As we pulled away,' recalled Chris, 'my mother turned to me and said, "I'm sorry, honey, but it was the only way." '

I told him, 'That's strange. Because those were almost the same words I used.'

He laughed. 'They're the same words all mothers use. They mean it, because they are sorry. And they are right, because it is the only way.'

I must say he seemed remarkably calm and as he talked on, Matteoni and the Moonies diminished into the distance.

Then he was asking, 'Does Sue ever have pillow fights with her brothers?'

And when I said she did, he smiled. 'Do you think it might help clear the air if I had a fight with her?'

I said, 'That just might be a really good idea. Sue's normally such an active girl that she must be terribly frustrated just sitting around doing nothing all day.'

Soon after we'd returned, Chris appeared in the sitting room carrying two pillows and threw one hard at Sue. 'Come on, hit me,' he said.

The speed of her reaction took him by surprise. The words had barely been spoken before she was attacking him with considerable vigour.

They had a tremendous stand-up fight with no quarter given while the rest of us retreated out of range. Eventually Sue and Chris collapsed exhausted. It had been great fun. And I found myself laughing for the first time since we'd heard about Brenna. She was laughing too and for one wild moment I thought it was all over, that the old Sue had come back. But even as I watched she was reverting to her Moonie self. It was as though the incident had never happened. Her face became trancelike and she was suddenly in another world.

Whenever we were alone Sue would say that she loved me and then repeat the line first spoken in the car on the day of the rescue: 'I feel so sorry for you, because you're going to be really hurt.'

Over and over again I would plead with her, 'Please just listen to what they have to say. Then you can make up your own mind.'

And each time she'd say, 'Mum, you just don't understand what's going on. These men are Satanic.'

Matthew had stressed that we were engaged in a race against time; and sometimes we didn't seem to be making any progress at all. But Matthew was comforting. 'She's probably doing more listening that we imagine,' he said. He smiled. 'English people have a reputation for being extra stubborn.'

We had one very bad moment when three police cars stopped just outside the motel. My heart just about stopped too. We tried to carry on as though totally unconcerned and they eventually took off, sirens at full blast. At almost any time of the day or night you could hear the sound of distant sirens. I would lay there in the darkness, hear them getting nearer, then going away again.

Matthew said it would be safer to pay by cash at the next motel, because we could then register with false names.

So the two of us drove down to the bank to cash some traveller's cheques, and ran into another crisis. The girl cashier asked for my passport. I handed it over, knowing that my name was in every newspaper in town. She took it into the manager's office and the minutes dragged by.

'It's just routine,' said Matthew, but I noticed that the fingers of that seemingly nerveless man had begun to tap on the counter.

She returned after an eternity with the money and the passport. And that night we travelled north in our new car and I began to breathe again.

SUSAN

I was angry with myself. I had let my shield slip during my fight with Chris and enjoyed the fun. Even worse I had found myself liking Chris. Now I felt really Fallen. Before I had become a Moonie, this had been the sort of man I fell for . . . good-looking, husky, charming and with a good sense of humour. But I had been warned so many times that Satan would use sex to lure me away from Father. So I had tried to hate him more than the others; and up until now it had worked.

Three days had gone by since they'd snatched me from the streets; and I still hadn't made any attempt to escape. But now that we were moving from the motel, I couldn't delay any longer. The next lodging place could be a room with bars, a cellar or they might even be planning to fly me out of the country.

Chris drove and as the speed rose I thought how easy it would be to grab the wheel and take the car off the road into the trees. A head-on collision would kill us all and make the most wonderful headlines for the Moonies. I would be a martyr and Father would redeem my soul. I pretended to be asleep and for a while the temptation to reach for the wheel was almost overpowering. Then I looked at my mother, sitting there with that peaceful look in her eyes, and suddenly I knew I couldn't go through with it. Not even for Father. So now there was only one choice left. I would make my escape bid as soon as we got out of the car. I had been so passive when arriving at the previous two motels that they might be taken unawares.

The journey took four hours and we pulled up outside yet another motel. I began to walk towards our new rooms with Dennis on one side, and Chris on the other. Then without any warning, I made my run.

I had gone just ten yards before Dennis, moving deceptively fast for such a big man, grabbed my left arm. Mark seized the other arm. Chris took my legs. And they carried me into the motel at a dead run. I screamed and in the quietness of the night, those screams should have woken the dead. But once again no one came to my rescue. Somebody clamped a hand over my mouth. Only this time I was fighting like a wildcat, scratching, kicking, driven on by desperation. I fought until I was totally exhausted. I was lying on the sitting-room carpet with

Chris and Dennis kneeling beside me. I had skinned both elbows and cut my mouth. Dennis was gently sponging away the blood and Chris was saying, 'Honey, why are you doing this to yourself? Can't you understand we only want to help you?'

This time there could be no doubt about the concern in his voice. It was there in his eyes too. And although I didn't realise it then the first chink of light was coming through.

We had been told so many times that deprogrammers were evil, Satanic people, that they would rape and torture us. But I knew that these men weren't evil. Misguided, yes, but not evil. I knew too that physically I had nothing to fear from them. They had no wish to harm me. They were kind, well-meaning men and it seemed so sad that they should have fallen under Satan's spell. I decided to pray for them.

ANNE

It was nice to wake up a long way from San Francisco, a long way from Matteoni. The motel was run by Indians who had probably never heard of the Moonies . . . or hopefully of kidnappings on the streets of the city.

We were still wearing the clothes that we'd worn when we first seized Sue, so it seemed high time for a change. I did the shopping for Sue and myself; and Matthew for the others. Sue changed into her new outfit only after I'd promised that I'd keep her dreadful Moonie clothes.

Chris and Mark had to leave us on the Saturday morning; and I felt as though I owed them both a debt I could never properly repay. With the vanity of a mother, I wished they could have stayed long enough to see the real Sue. I was sure they would have liked her that much more.

I said so to Chris and he laughed.

'Aren't you forgetting something?' he said. 'Remember I walked that same long road.'

SUSAN

A new guard, big and burly, had been hired that morning. He was sitting in a chair beside the door, reading a book. We were alone and I knew I would never have a better chance of making my escape. I would have to crash through the glass. There was no other way. My first plan was to grab the curtain rail and swing feet first through the window. But I discarded that, because the rail didn't look strong enough to support my weight. So I decided to dive head-first through the glass, somersault, land on my feet beside the cars parked in the street below and then run.

I climbed off the bed slowly. The guard glanced at me casually and just as casually I stretched and yawned. He turned the page of his book; and at that moment I took two strides and dived. My head struck the glass with the most fearsome crash and I bounced straight back into the room to fall semi-conscious upon the floor.

I was vaguely aware of the guard shouting, my mother's anguished cry and Dennis's big hands upon me.

'If that glass had broken,' said the guard, sounding shaken, 'she'd have killed herself out there.'

My mother was saying, 'Oh, dear God, is she hurt?'

And Dennis in that quiet voice of his replied, 'It's okay. There's a bump coming up, nothing else.'

He carried me as easily as though I'd been a baby and placed me on the bed. He ran a hand down the side of my face.

'You great dummy,' he said, but the hand and the voice were gentle and I was astonished to see the hint of tears in his eyes.

ANNE

I felt so shattered that Sue could take such a risk just to get away from us. It seemed as though we hadn't made any progress at all. But to my surprise Matthew was smiling.

'Believe me,' he said, 'that's the beginning of the end. The Moonies programme them to destruct when the truth is starting to get through. That was the last fling. Very soon now it will all be over.'

Meanwhile Inspector Al Matteoni had sent a message to Michael via Scotland Yard. Would he please ring San Francisco? And being a cautious man Michael took notes of the conversation that followed. They make interesting reading. This is the way they went:

Michael: This is Michael Swatland ringing from England as requested.

Matteoni: I've been trying to get you all week. Your number is out of order or something.

Michael: My telephone is all right, but callers from America are finding it difficult to get through.

Matteoni: Has your wife called?

Michael: Yes. Both my wife and daughter are fine.

Matteoni: Only I would like to speak to her myself.

Michael: I get the impression from reading the newspapers that you would like to do more than just *talk* to my wife.

Matteoni: What do you mean?

Michael: I am talking about the kidnapping charge, ten years imprisonment, and all that.

Matteoni: You can't believe everything that's written in the papers. Reporters have got to earn their bread.

Michael: Several of the stories quote you directly on that point.

Matteoni: I only want to make sure that your daughter is okay and wants to return to England with her mother under her own free-will.

Michael: You seem to be going about it in a mighty queer way. Hunting them down like criminals. Combing every hotel and motel in San Francisco. Allowing the Moonies to join in the hunt. I'm beginning to wonder whose side you are on.

Matteoni: Mr Swatland, I know how you feel. I'm a family man myself. Your wife and daughter are a long way from home. All I want them to do is call in and see me.

Michael: My wife and daughter are no longer in the city. But I understand that my daughter will be signing a paper in the presence of a lawyer, stating that she wishes to return to England with her mother. And a copy of that statement will be sent to you in San Francisco.

Matteoni: You must realise that your wife and daughter cannot leave the States without my say so.

Michael: As I understand it, a signed statement in the presence of a lawyer is good enough to get them home.

Matteoni: No, you are wrong there. They need my consent. All they have to do is come and see me and if I'm satisfied that your daughter is okay and wants to go home with her mother, then they will be free to go. I won't press any kidnapping charges on your wife. I'll even take them to the airport and kiss 'em both goodbye.

I didn't make any attempt to contact Matteoni, because there was too much mystery wrapped around him. He had used almost those selfsame words to the Steinbergs; and then returned Brenna to the Moonies where she may well remain for the rest of her days.

I had no means of knowing whether he was a family man (as he claimed) touched by the fate of children in the cult . . . a hunter who would use any means to catch his prey . . . or simply a policeman caught up in the conflict of statutory law and moral justice.

All I did know was that, with Sue's entire future at stake, it was a risk I just didn't dare take.

Chapter Fifteen

RETURN OF A DAUGHTER

'One day you'll look back and all this will seem no more than a distant dream.' Dennis

ANNE

DENNIS HAD been talking to Sue on and off for five days; and for much of that time he must have felt as though he was talking to a statue. Today appeared to be following the same pattern as the ones that had gone before. Dennis talked in his quiet, patient way and Sue's eyes remained fixed on some faraway horizon. Then all of a sudden she returned and looked at him.

'You know something,' she said and she was smiling, 'you're cute.'

She was gently teasing him and it was so unexpected that Dennis was briefly lost for words. Then the big grin came. 'I guess I've been called some things in my time,' he said. 'But I don't recollect ever being called cute before.'

Everyone was smiling. And that was the moment when I finally knew the old Sue was coming back. This was a reminder of the lighthearted days before she walked into the Kingdom of the Moon. I gave her a hug and a kiss; something I had done several times in the past few days without getting any response at all. This time she hugged and kissed me in return, and it was a lovely feeling.

The transformation that followed moved slowly. She still thought we were mistaken; but now she was listening, talking, thinking . . . and that's all we'd ever asked.

Chris and Mark had been replaced by Michael and Virginia; and again we couldn't have hoped for better people. Michael, bearded and dark, was a quiet man. A very caring person who'd achieved a position of power in the Moonies until rescued by his parents. Virginia, tall, dark and warm, was another ex-Moonie. She had the most amazing laugh, very contagious. And soon Sue was talking to them both quite freely.

On the brink of midnight with everything going so well, we heard the wail of police sirens. We had heard them many times before and they had all gone by. But this time the car turned into the forecourt of the motel and stopped outside our door, lights still flashing, siren still wailing. I was quite sure it had come for us . . . and that, as in the case of Brenna, it had come a day too soon. Sue could still snap back so easily. I was in the kitchen with Dennis and we both froze. Matthew and Michael were talking quietly to Sue in the next room and I'm sure they must have been feeling bad too. I could picture all of us in jail and even worse, Sue back in the Moonies.

I prayed silently, 'Please make them go. Please don't let them come here.'

Dennis didn't say a word. He just reached out and took my hand into that huge paw. And I'd never been in greater need of comfort. We stayed like that, scarcely daring to breathe, for fully a minute. Then suddenly there was a tremendous commotion outside, shouts in Spanish, the sounds of a struggle, car doors slamming, engine revving, wheels beginning to turn, and slowly the truth dawned. The police had arrested the people next door. We were told later that they were illegal immigrants. To hear those sirens disappearing into the night was very literally the answer to a prayer.

The following day was Sunday and we were all beginning to feel light-headed. She wasn't just listening. She was asking questions and clearly starting to show doubts.

She said to Matthew, 'I will listen to you for three days and you will have to convince me by then, But I don't want to hear any more of those beastly tapes. Just talk to me instead.'

Matthew smiled. 'All right,' he said, 'no tapes, that's a promise. They get in the way of a conversation.'

I left them all talking together and went into the next room. Now that it was almost over I felt so tired. Every now and then Sue's laugh would ring out and to me it was the sweetest music. I closed my eyes and when I opened them Dennis was standing beside me.

'How do you feel now?' he asked.

I said, 'I feel so drained, as though I have no feelings left after all that's happened. Does that make any kind of sense?'

He nodded his big shaggy head. 'You've been through a rough time,' he said. 'But one day you'll look back and all this will seem no more than a distant dream.'

Some time later I phoned Lea to tell her that Sue had seen the truth at last and asked her to give the good news to Michael. I was still being very wary. There had been something strange about our phone at home all week.

I sensed that in so many ways Michael must have gone through the toughest time of all. I knew that he would much rather have been in America, helping with the rescue. And loving Sue as he did, the waiting and the worrying must have been sheer torture.

Monday was to be the team's last day together. Sue had made such rapid progress that she would be going to the rehabilitation centre on the Tuesday. For the moment her main desire was to return to San Francisco in a bid to get all her friends out of the cult. Matthew, both amused and touched, suggested that we should maybe wait a week or two before setting up this mass exodus.

We celebrated with an evening meal at a restaurant. We were all there, Matthew, Dennis, Michael, Virginia, Sue and myself; and it seemed incredible that so much could have happened, so much could have changed, in the space of a week.

Just seven days earlier we had snatched a stranger from the streets of San Francisco. Now she was a stranger no more.

✿

It was Saturday and Matthew was saying, 'Sue, let's make a deal. Listen to us for three days and listen with an open mind. And then after that you can make your own free choice. You can decide to either stay or leave. If you want to walk out of that door, no one will try to stop you. Just so long as you play fair first and really listen. Now what do you say?'

I agreed, because it all seemed so easy. All I had to do was listen for three days and then return to Bush Street. I was confident that my faith would hold. To convince Matthew that I was cooperating, I wrote out a lot of questions mostly about Moon's interpretation of the Bible. I began to talk freely and to listen; and once a Moonie begins to do that, it's all over. The Divine Principle, the whole basis of the Unification Church, falls apart. And that is why Moonies need to be programmed. Without the indoctrination camps, it would be a very small and lonely faith.

By Sunday afternoon, I had come to realise that I had been brainwashed or at least placed under mind control . . . and by the evening I had made the firm decision that my Moonie days were over. But having accepted the fact that I'd been duped left a sadness in its wake. How about all the brothers and sisters I'd come to love? Knowing that they had been duped too, had I the right to just walk away and leave them? I even thought seriously about returning to Bush Street, telling everyone I had escaped and then working from the inside to warn people. It was, of course, an impossible dream; but you have to remember that my mind had been in prison for eight months. It was still a little lost in the outside world.

Our farewell meal was really my first contact with that outside world since the day I'd wandered into that spider's web known as Bush Street. It seemed so strange to be free, to enjoy myself without feeling selfish, to look around at fellow diners and not condemn them for being Fallen or Satanic.

It was Tuesday and the time for goodbyes. We all drove down to the airport at Sacramento and Dennis was the first to leave. He was going home to his wife and family.

I said, 'I just don't know how to thank you. Words seem so inadequate.'

He looked across at Susan who was laughing, sharing some joke with Virginia, and then he smiled slowly. 'On a day such as this,' he said, 'who needs thanks?'

He gave us each a quick hug and then he was striding away through the crowd. I was reminded once again of all those Western heroes I'd seen on the silver screen. By then we had all grown very fond of Dennis which wasn't difficult. He was an easy man to like.

We said goodbye to Virginia and I only wished we'd had time to know her better. She seemed such fun.

And then Matthew, Michael, Sue and I flew east to the Rehab. We travelled as Matthew's wife and mother. We hadn't forgotten that the police were still looking for us. Nor had we forgotten how much we owed Matthew. His careful planning had saved us at Walnut Creek and continued to keep trouble at bay in those vital days that followed.

While Sue settled in happily at the Rehab, I was taken in by an American couple nearby who were kindness itself. Sue signed an affidavit* designed to legalise the actions of the rescue team. But I still felt like a fugitive. I jumped every time the phone rang and police sirens continued to chill the blood.

At seven-thirty on the evening of 6 April, 1981, Sue and I flew out of New York's Kennedy Airport. I watched the skyscrapers until distance had diminished them to mere dots on the horizon. And then, and only then, did I feel safe. The adventure was over. We were coming home.

**See* Appendix 3, page 151.

CONCLUSION

SUSAN

Sometimes I look back upon it all as a distant nightmare; something that happened to somebody else, a stranger I barely knew. I'm told that this is the defence mechanism of the mind. For it's not pleasant to realise that you've been hoodwinked, that your most precious ideals have been violated, that you've followed a false God. I am still bitter, but my bitterness is reserved solely for the Reverend Moon and the entourage which surrounds him. The rank and file Moonies, and many of their leaders too, were some of the nicest people I have ever known. Nice people who had been programmed to do terrible things. Despite the sham, the trickery and the tears, my eight months in the Moonies were not entirely wasted ones. I found a love amongst my fellow victims deeper than anything I have encountered in any other group before or since.

Maybe there is a message here for the established churches. Maybe they would do well to search their own hearts and their own consciences. If they could promote a similar love within their own congregations, the main appeal of the Moonies for my own generation would disappear. It's hard to peddle dreams to people who have already seen their dreams come true.

ANNE

In a perfect world, it shouldn't be necessary for a mother to take her daughter by force from the city streets. But then in a perfect world there would be no place for millionaire messiahs who use deceit and mind control to lure the young away from their families. And until governments exercise some control over quasi-religious cults such as the Moonies, parents will continue to find themselves in that grey area where moral justice conflicts so strangely with the law of the land. We are told that senate sub-committees will eventually be set up in the United States to study this late twentieth-century phenomenon. But surely plain old-fashioned commonsense would serve a better purpose.

If the Unification Church can only operate by trickery . . . or to use its own phrase, by Heavenly Deception . . . there has to be something terribly wrong with this so-called church and with the laws which currently protect it.

We can count ourselves as the lucky ones. Our daughter has come home. Our family is now closer knit than ever before. We have been touched by the faith of friends and humbled by the kindness of strangers. This may not be a perfect world, but it is nevertheless a much better place than we had hitherto believed it to be.

APPENDIX 1

MOONIES' GLOSSARY

Actionise. To work on behalf of the cult with total dedication. This normally involves selling on the streets or recruiting new members.

Blessing. This is a marriage arranged and conducted by the Reverend Sun Myung Moon. Moonies are normally only allowed to marry after they achieve 'purity' with a minimum six-year spell in the Unification Church. They must only marry one another; because in this way they will raise 'perfect' children.

Brother. Officially any male Moonie is a brother. But in practice this term only applies to rank and file members, not to the hierarchy.

Center Man. Anyone who controls the actions of others in the cult. It particularly applies to the policy makers.

Cereal Drama. Group session during breakfast in which new members are encouraged to talk about their past life. This is an important facet of indoctrination; because their more intimate confessions are used to produce feelings of guilt.

Chants. The Moonie Chants have little in common with the Chants normally associated with monasteries. Moonie Chants are used as part of the indoctrination system to blank out independent thinking.

Chooch. A ritual chant in which the Moonies link arms and shout, 'Choo-choo-choo, choo-choo-choo. Yea! Yea! Pow!' They are acting out a Christmas story when the presents had to be taken over the top of a mountain to reach the children in a village on the other side. All the big trains had broken down. So a little engine nobly took on the task. He choo-choo-chooed up the mountain and the 'Pow!' is a cry of triumph as he reaches the top.

Chosen. People who are considered so spiritual that they are supposedly directed into the Unification Church by God himself.

Clunk-it. Going to bed and falling asleep instantly. The Moonies disapprove of their members lying awake.

Fallen World. This is the entire human race with the notable exception of the Moonies who alone can find salvation. An essential part of their doctrine is that Satan seduced Eve and therefore tainted the blood of us all.

Family. The membership of the Unification Church.

Father. One of the titles by which the Reverend Sun Myung Moon is known to his followers.

Heavenly Deception. Because the Moonies believe that the outside world is evil, they see nothing wrong in deceiving that evil world . . . providing that this is done for the benefit of the Unification Church.

Heavenly Father. The Moonies' name for God. A typical prayer will begin 'Dear Heavenly Father and then the word 'Father' will be used repeatedly. Confusion occurs and many Moonies believe they are praying to Moon.

Hi-vival. An evangelical spectacular usually built around the Church's President, Mose Durst.

Holy Days. The Moonies celebrate four Holy Days . . . God's Day, True Parents Day, Children's Day, and World Day. They pay little attention to either Christmas or Easter.

Horizontal Relationships. Friendships between members on the same spiritual plane. These are discouraged in the Moonies. Love is supposed to be lavished upon the entire group and not upon one particular individual. Ultimate love must be reserved for the Messiah, namely the Reverend Moon.

Indemnity. The Moonies believe that we are all ancestors of Satan and must therefore pay a debt to God (our indemnity) before we can be saved. This can be achieved by constant obedience, love and sacrifice; and in certain very special ways . . . such as by bringing 360 (a supposedly magical number) of recruits into the movement.

Jump-it. The opposite to Clunk-it. Waking up and getting out of bed instantly.

Love Bombing. Constant open affection directed towards a new recruit by the rest of the group. Designed to overwhelm; and frequently used when the recruit threatens to leave the cult.

Matched. This is an engagement arranged by the Reverend Moon. He says that he can select perfect partners by studying the way they talk, the way they smile. The partners have often never met before the matching and frequently belong to different countries and different races. The matching can normally only occur after the brother and sister have spent three years in the Moonies; and then a further three years must go by before they can be blessed.

Oatmealing. Negative talking or saying bad things about the Family.

Red Robin. The person responsible for waking up his or her fellow Moonies each morning.

Restoring. Recruiting, the essence of which is to 'restore' purity to the soul.

Sleepy Spirits. The evil spirits which try to send brothers and sisters to sleep during the daytime, especially during lectures.

Spacing Out. Day dreaming.

Spirit Man. The Moonies believe in the existence of a Spirit World which only Moon can control. So the cult Spirit Man takes over whenever a Moonie suffers physical death and goes to the kingdom controlled by his Messiah.

Spiritual Age. Judged on the time in which you have been in the Unification Church. In other words, you have your third birthday three years after joining.

Spiritual Child. Anyone recruited becomes the Spiritual Child of the restorer who brought him or her into the Moonies. Thus Susan regarded Eric as her Spiritual Father.

Trinity. Small sub-families in the centres.

True Parents. The Reverend Moon and his wife Hak Ja-Han who is known as 'The Mother of the Universe'.

Witnessing. Another word for recruiting or restoring.

APPENDIX 2

The United States Congress asked the Fraser Committee on International Organisations to investigate Korean-American relations. The following statement by the Committee's Staff Director Robert Boettcher was made on 15 November, 1979:

The ritual death of more than nine hundred Americans in Guyana last year unfortunately did not lead to an awakened national concern about destructive religious cults. Instead the tragedy came and went as just a media event. Its place in the public consciousness today seems mainly to be as one of the 'big stories' of 1978. Americans seem unprepared to come to grips with the possibility that there are other Jim Joneses whose words are absolute to large followings, and who operate as if above the law and with frightening potential for violence and death.

Our institutions, such as the mental health establishment and law enforcement agencies, fail to address seriously the phenomenon revealed by the People's Temple. Yet it is still with us. The cults are flourishing. The one I know best . . . the organisation of Sun Myung Moon . . . has in the past two years expanded its business empire with fishing industries in five states and the backing of a movie starring Laurence Olivier and Jacqueline Bisset. Only three months ago, two Moonies were charged with firing shots into an occupied car, an act of violence defended by a Unification Church spokesperson. And next week in Los Angeles, Moon will hold his annual International Conference for the Unity of the Sciences. Each year, hundreds of scientists and scholars, some of them Nobel laureates, attend the conference, even knowing that Moon intends to use them for his own propaganda, that he tells his obedient followers, 'I am your brain,' and that former members of the cult say Moon preaches and teaches suicide.

The people are entitled to an active interest in the cult phenomenon by mental health and behavioral professionals. One Harvard psychiatrist has said cult indoctrination techniques are 'direct assaults on sanity.' Ex-Moonies have said they felt capable of killing their parents and old friends while in the cult. But there are very few professionals studying cult mind control. They seem unprepared to deal with the concept, and the National Institute of Mental Health has been deterred even from discussing it by angry objections from the cults themselves.

An important legal question is also being ignored. There are compelling arguments that cult mind control violates the Thirteenth Amendment of the Constitution, which outlaws involuntary servitude.

As long as there is no accepted definition, scientific or legal, of mind control, cult leaders can continue to do their worst to recruits, efforts to free persons from cults will stay mired in legal controversy, and constructive treatment of former members will be hard to come by.

Inaction by the Justice Department has been characterised by confusion, caution, and neglect. For confusion, we have Attorney General Bell's comment after the Guyana tragedy: 'I don't know what a cult is. I'm a Baptist. Maybe I'm a member of a cult.' Then two months later Bell said he believed Patty Hearst had been brainwashed, but did nothing to suggest he thought brainwashing was possible by anyone other than Patty Hearst's captors.

For caution, there is a letter to a Congressman by Benjamin Civiletti before he became Attorney General. On behalf of the Justice Department, he refused to look into the coercive effects of brainwashing because, he said, to do so 'would seem to require a finding that the members' religious beliefs were false.' Earlier, during the Ford administration, the Justice Department turned down a State Department request to investigate Moon's Unification Church for the reason that there was no prima facie evidence that it was not a bona fide church.

All of these attitudes play into the hands of the Moon cult which, for convenience sake, began calling itself a church about ten years ago and, ever since, has been insisting deceitfully and successfully that it is really no different from the established churches and therefore must have full First Amendment protection.

For neglect, we have the Justice Department ignoring the evidence and recommendations of the Fraser subcommittee, of which Congressman Leo Ryan, slain in Guyana, was a member. As stated in the final report of its Investigation of Korean-American Relations in 1978, the subcommittee found evidence that the Moon Organisation had systematically violated US laws governing taxes, immigration, banking, currency, and foreign agents registration, and had at least attempted to violate the Arms Export Control Act in connection with Moon's manufacture of M-16 rifles at his armaments plant in Korea.

Since the subcommittee's mandate had expired and it had no law enforcement authority, it recommended that the executive branch of the federal government form an interagency task force to examine the evidence and conduct further investigation to determine whether formal charges should be brought by the appropriate agencies. A year later the Justice Department, whose role would be central in such a task force, has taken no action other than to decide against the task force proposal.

Some specifics on the Justice Department's neglect:

The subcommittee found evidence that the Moon Organisation had acted as an unregistered agent of the South Korean government by organising political demonstrations for the Korean CIA, collecting money in the United States to support a radio service controlled by the Korean CIA, and negotiating with Americans for renewal of a Korean government contract to make M-16 rifles.

The only action known to have been taken by the Justice Department was in 1971 when it conducted one interview with Bo Hi Pak, Moon's chief minion in

Washington. Pak was asked if he was a Korean agent, said he was not, and Justice closed the case.

The Immigration and Naturalisation Service, which is subordinate to Justice, apparently has done nothing with evidence that Moon and his wife may be illegal aliens. There is a strong indication that they obtained their immigrant visas by making false statements.

The FBI, also in Justice's domain, could be expected to investigate thoroughly and make findings about an organisation operating throughout the country whose leader's speeches are replete with exhortations of death and violence, and whose members have fomented violence and been reported to have made numerous death threats. There are no indications that the FBI is doing so with respect to the Moonies.

The FBI and Justice Department action which led to convicting nine Scientologists of conspiracy seems only minimally encouraging for the general public and somewhat ironic. In this case, the government did move against cult lawlessness, but it was for the purpose of protecting the government's own particular interests, since the Scientologists had broken into government offices and planted spies in government agencies.

Moon's ties with the Korean government having been ignored by the Justice Department, the prospects for his future relations with the Korean government may be brighter than ever. The person emerging as likely to succeed President Park Chung Hee as the new strong man is Kim Jong Pil, the founder of the Korean CIA. For the past seventeen years, Kim has been Moon's most influential political ally.

The former members of Moon's cult who are here today deserve support for the organisation they have founded, Ex-Members Against Moon. I know they have a sincere motivation to help persons still under Moon's control, who are bright, able young men and women like themselves.

The American people deserve support from the government, mental health professionals, and media.

Lawlessness and psychological abuse, whether practiced by the Mafia or self-styled messiahs, should be put down. Jim Jones had his last stand in the Guyana jungle. Moon tells his followers he has an island off the coast of South Korea where he will take them when the world turns against him. One Jonestown tragedy is one too many.

APPENDIX 3

AFFIDAVIT

To whom it may concern:

I Susan Swatland having learned that my leaving San Francisco so abruptly has caused considerable confusion. I have had this affidavit prepared so that I might set the record straight without having to personally return to San Francisco, where I have left behind old problems and a way of life which I dearly wish to forget.

To the police and all other legal agencies I want to emphasise that I have not been abducted nor am I being held against my will. I am presently travelling with my mother and some friends, and soon I will be returning to my home in England. Additionally in order to clarify to anyone concerned, I am free to return to San Francisco or to go anywhere else that I may choose.

My leaving San Francisco at this time was so I could be with my mother and to get away from the Unification Church. Further I wish to make my position clear to the Unification Church, its members and agents, that I do not wish to be contacted by them in any manner. Should I desire contact in the future with the Unification Church or its members I will initiate the contact. Finally to those people who have helped me leave San Francisco, I wish to thank them and to express my hope that their help has not caused them to have trouble with the police, the courts or the Unification Church.

Dated 26 March, 1981 *Susan Swatland*

APPENDIX 4

FRONT ORGANISATIONS

The Unification Church operates under an umbrella of front organisations.

The following information was supplied by members and ex-members of the Unification Church.

FRONT NAMES USED BY THE UNIFICATION CHURCH IN NORTH AMERICA

BUSINESS FRONTS

Aladdins Coffees, Teas and Kindreds
Boston Principle Company
Canaan Health Foods
Christian Bernard Jewellery
Far Eastern Travel Agency, New York
Hsu and Company, Columbus, Ohio
Il Shin Stoneworks Company
Il Wha American Corporation
Il Wha Ginseng Center, New York
Il Wha Ginseng Company, Cleveland, Ohio
Il Wha Pharmaceutical Company
International Exchange Maintenance, San Francisco
International Exchange Union, San Francisco
International Karate School (over 2,000 schools in America)
International Seafood Enterprises, New York
Jusancha Ginseng Tea
Oceanic Seafood Enterprises, New York
One Mind Enterprises, Mibrae, California
Original World Products, New York
Rising Tide Bookstore, Washington DC
Rose Shop, Leamington Hotel, Oakland, California
Seno Travel Service, San Francisco
Sky Valley Ranch, Kalkaska, Michigan
Sun Deli, New York and Washington DC
Sunny Nature, Detroit, Michigan

Tae Han Rutile Company
Taiyo, Atlanta
Tong il Enterprises, New York
Tong il Industries International
Tong Wha Titanium Company
Tree of Life (microbiotic restaurant) New York
US Marine Enterprises
Whole Earth and Unity Incorporated, Cleveland, Ohio

RELIGIOUS FRONTS

Celebration of Life
The Holy Spirit Association for the Unification of World Christianity
Interfaith Endeavour
International One World Crusade
Jewish Friendship League
Judaism: In Service to the World
Sun Myung Moon Christian Crusade
The Unification Church
Unification Theological Seminary, Barrytown, New York
The Unified Family

POLITICAL FRONTS

American Bicentennial God Bless America Committee
American Committeee for Human Rights of Japanese Wives of North Korean Repatriates
American Council for World Freedom, Washington DC
American Youth for a Just Peace
Captive Nations
Committee for Responsible Dialogue
Freedom Leadership Foundation
International Federation for the Victory over Communism
Korean-American Political Association
National Prayer and Fast Committee for the Watergate Crisis
Professors Academy for World Peace
Project Unity

World Anti-Communist League
World Freedom Institute

RECRUITING FRONTS

Collegiate Association for the Research of Principles
Creative Community Project
Eden Awareness Training Center
Day of Hope Festival
Day of Hope Tour
Divine Principle Home Study Course
High School Association for the Research of Principles
International Foundation for the Advancement of Biological Medicine
International Friendship Banquet
International Ideal City Project/Ranch, San Francisco
International Leadership Seminar
International Pioneer Academy
International Prisoner Re-education Foundation
International Re-education Foundation, San Francisco
New Education Development Systems Incorporated
Students for an Ethical Society
UNI-CAP, Community Action Programme, California
Unification Thought Institute
US Youth Council
World Family Movement
World of Hope Festival
World Mission Center . . . New Yorker Hotel

CULTURAL FRONTS

Center for Ethical Management and Planning, Berkeley
Children's Relief Fund
Council on Unified Research of Science
DC Striders Track Club
Ethics and the Environment Conference
Go World Brass Band
International Conference for the Unity of the Sciences
International Cultural Foundation
International Folk Ballet

Japanese Cultural Foundation
Korean Cultural and Freedom Foundation
Korean Folk Ballet
Little Angels Korean Folk Ballet
New Age Orchestra, San Francisco
New Age Players, Theatrical Company, New York
New Hope Singers International
New York City Symphony
Re-education Band, Berkeley
Sunburst (rock group)
Voices of Freedom (rock group) Washington DC

MEDIA FRONTS

Epoch Maker, magazine
International Exchange Press
Manhattan, magazine
Manhattan Television Center, 311 West 34th Street, New York
New Future Films
New Hope News
New World Communications Incorporated, daily newspaper
One Way Productions Incorporated
Principle Life
Queens, magazine
Renaissance for resources
Rising Tide, weekly by Freedom Leadership Foundation (political)
Spring of Life, nutrition journal
Sunrise, newsletter
Tong-il Seigel, monthly, Japanese
Universal Voice, newspaper
Way of the World, monthly magazine
The Weekly Religion
World Daily News, daily

MOONIE CENTERS IN USA

New York

Dr Mose Durst
4 West 53rd Street,
New York 10036
212-997-1072

34th Street and 8th Avenue,
World Mission Center.
(previously the New Yorker Hotel)

Down Town Inn, a café of sorts to which new recruits are taken. It is situated around the corner from the World Mission Center.

4 West 43rd Street.
(previously the Columbia Alumni Club)

Moonies recruit regularly in front of the library on 5th Avenue near the 43rd Street address. They usually operate under the banners of Camp New Hope and Project Volunteer.

San Francisco

Centers in the Bay Area are usually referred to as the Creative Community Project, Project Volunteer or New Education Development Systems (NEDS).

1153 Bush Street,
San Francisco, CA 94115.
415-928-9607
282-3603
474-0724

2649 Washington Street,
San Francisco, CA 94119
415-563-9411
567-3468

2717 Hearst Street,
Berkeley, CA 94709
415-548-3184

2955 Ashby Street,
Berkeley, CA 94709
415-549-3264

6502 Dana Street,
Oakland, CA
415-654-6826

International Exchange Maintenance
(Carpet Cleaning Company),
880 81st Avenue,
Oakland, CA
415-632-6200
(the minimum activities of Project Volunteer are also carried on here. It is also known as the Ideal Street Warehouse)

Camp A (Aetna Springs),
near Pope Valley, CA
707-965-3621

Camp K,
near Calistoga, CA, on route 128
707-433-9996
433-3927

Boonville,
near Boonville, CA, on route 128
(also called the Ideal City Ranch)
707-895-9933

Los Angeles

5561 Huntington Drive,
Los Angeles, CA
714-338-2116

Camp Mazundar,
near San Bernadino, CA
714-338-2116

APPENDIX 5

FOR FURTHER INFORMATION AND ADVICE

In America

American Family Foundation Inc.,
P.O. Box 343,
Lexington,
Massachusetts MA 02173

Citizens Freedom Foundation Information Service,
P.O. Box 7000-89,
1719 Via El Prado,
Redondo Beach,
California 90277

Ex-Members Against Moon,
P.O. Box 62,
Brootline,
Massachusetts 02146

In England

EMERGE (Ex-Members of Extremist Religious Groups),
BCM Box 1199,
London WC1N 3XX.

FAIR (Family Action, Information and Rescue),
BCM Box 3535, P.O. Box 12,
London WC1N 3XX.